easy to make!
One Pot

Good Housekeeping

easy to make!
One Pot

COLLINS & BROWN

First published in Great Britain in 2008
by Collins & Brown
10 Southcombe Street
London W14 0RA

An imprint of Anova Books Company Ltd.

The Good Housekeeping website is
www.allaboutyou.com/goodhousekeeping

10 9 8 7 6 5 4

ISBN 978-1-84340-447-7

A catalogue record for this book is available from the British
Library.

Reproduction by Dot Gradations Ltd
Printed and bound by Times Offset (M) Sdn. Bhd, Malaysia

Keep updated. Email food@anovabooks.com

This book can be ordered direct from the publisher at
www.anovabooks.com

NOTES

- Both metric and imperial measures are given for the recipes. Follow either set of measures, not a mixture of both, as they are not interchangeable.
- All spoon measures are level.
  1 tsp = 5ml spoon; 1 tbsp = 15ml spoon.
- Ovens and grills must be preheated to the specified temperature.
- Use sea salt and freshly ground black pepper unless otherwise suggested.
- Fresh herbs should be used unless dried herbs are specified in a recipe.
- Medium eggs should be used except where otherwise specified. Free-range eggs are recommended.
- Note that certain recipes, including mayonnaise, lemon curd and some cold desserts, contain raw or lightly cooked eggs. The young, elderly, pregnant women and anyone with an immune-deficiency disease should avoid these, because of the slight risk of salmonella.
- Calorie, fat and carbohydrate counts per serving are provided for the recipes.
- If you are following a gluten- or dairy-free diet, check the labels on all pre-packaged food goods.
- Nutritional information for serving suggestions do not take gluten- or dairy-free diets into account.

Picture Credits
Photographers: Nicki Dowey (pages 32, 38, 60, 64, 66, 70, 73, 75, 76, 78, 80, 86, 91, 111); Craig Robertson (all other photography)
Stylist: Helen Trent
Home Economist: Anna Burges-Lumsden

Contents

Foreword

Cooking in one pot is a very creative way of making a meal, and not just the preserve of campers and students with neither the space nor the cash to splash out on lots of equipment. It's energy-efficient, too – and with fewer pans to wash up, you can save up to two litres of water going down the drain. In *One Pot* we explore techniques from stir-frying to slow-cooking, concluding with some tempting desserts.

Soups and stews, where anything can be added to the pot, lend themselves brilliantly to this style of cooking. We've included recipes for traditional casseroles that you just pop in the oven for an hour or two, as well as some wonderful rice dishes from around the world, such as paella from Spain, jambalaya from Louisiana and Caribbean chicken.

Need to rustle up a quick midweek supper? Try prawns in yellow bean sauce, a flash-in-the-pan Asian-style dish that's ready in less than half an hour. Or try chicken, bean and spinach curry, which just needs a warmed naan bread to serve alongside. And in the recipe for spicy sausage and pasta supper you don't need an extra pan of boiling water to cook the pasta; because all the ingredients are cooked in one pan, the individual flavours combine to produce a delicious meal.

These are just a few of my favourites from the 101 ideas featured in this book. All the recipes have been triple-tested in the Good Housekeeping kitchens to make sure they work every time.

Emma

Emma Marsden
Cookery Editor
Good Housekeeping

0

The Basics

Making stock

Good stock can make the difference between a good dish and a great one. It gives depth of flavour to many dishes. There are four main types of stock: vegetable, meat, chicken and fish.

Cook's Tips

- To get a clearer liquid when making fish, meat or poultry stock, strain the cooked stock through four layers of muslin in a sieve.
- Stock will keep for three days in the refrigerator. If you want to keep it for a further three days, transfer it to a pan and reboil gently for five minutes. Cool, put in a clean bowl and chill for a further three days.
- When making meat or chicken stock, make sure there is a good ratio of meat to bones. The more meat you use, the more flavour the stock will have.

Stocks

Vegetable Stock

For 1.2 litres (2 pints), you will need:
225g (8oz) each onions, celery, leeks and carrots, chopped, 2 bay leaves, a few thyme sprigs, 1 small bunch parsley, 10 black peppercorns, ½ tsp salt.

1   Put all the ingredients in a large pan and add 1.7 litres (3 pints) cold water. Bring slowly to the boil and skim the surface.

2   Partially cover the pan and simmer for 30 minutes. Adjust the seasoning if necessary. Strain the stock through a fine sieve into a bowl and leave to cool.

Meat Stock

For 900ml (1½ pints), you will need:
450g (1lb) each meat bones and stewing meat, 1 onion, 2 celery sticks and 1 large carrot, sliced, 1 bouquet garni (2 bay leaves, a few thyme sprigs and a small bunch parsley), 1 tsp black peppercorns, ½ tsp salt.

1   Preheat the oven to 220°C (200°C fan oven) mark 7. Put the meat and bones in a roasting tin and roast for 30–40 minutes, turning now and again, until they are well browned.

2   Put the bones in a large pan with the remaining ingredients and add 2 litres (3½ pints) cold water. Bring slowly to the boil and skim the surface.

3   Partially cover the pan and simmer for 4–5 hours. Adjust the seasoning if necessary. Strain through a muslin-lined sieve into a bowl and cool quickly. Degrease (see opposite) before using.

Chicken Stock

For 1.2 litres (2 pints), you will need:
1.6kg (3½lb) chicken bones, 225g (8oz) each onions
and celery, sliced, 150g (5oz) chopped leeks,
1 bouquet garni (2 bay leaves, a few thyme sprigs
and a small bunch parsley), 1 tsp black peppercorns,
½ tsp salt.

1 Put all the ingredients in a large pan and add
3 litres (5¼ pints) cold water. Bring slowly to
the boil and skim the surface.

2 Partially cover the pan and simmer gently for
2 hours. Adjust the seasoning if necessary.

3 Strain the stock through a muslin-lined
sieve into a bowl and cool quickly. Degrease
(see right) before using.

Fish Stock

For 900ml (1½ pints), you will need:
900g (2lb) fish bones and trimmings, washed,
2 carrots, 1 onion and 2 celery sticks, sliced,
1 bouquet garni (2 bay leaves, a few thyme sprigs
and a small bunch parsley), 6 white peppercorns,
½ tsp salt.

1 Put all the ingredients in a large pan and add
900ml (1½ pints) cold water. Bring slowly to
the boil and skim the surface.

2 Partially cover the pan and simmer gently for
30 minutes. Adjust the seasoning if necessary.

3 Strain through a muslin-lined sieve into a bowl
and cool quickly. Fish stock tends not to have
much fat in it and so does not usually need to
be degreased. However, if it does seem to be
fatty, you will need to remove this by
degreasing it (see right).

Degreasing stock

Meat and poultry stock needs to be degreased. (Vegetable
stock does not.) You can mop the fat from the surface
using kitchen paper, but the following methods are easier
and more effective. There are three main methods that you
can use: ladling, pouring and chilling.

1 **Ladling** While the stock is warm, place a ladle on
the surface. Press down and allow the fat floating on
the surface to trickle over the edge until the ladle is
full. Discard the fat, then repeat until all the fat has
been removed.

2 **Pouring** For this you need a degreasing jug or a
double-pouring gravy boat, which has the spout
at the base of the vessel. When you fill the jug or
gravy boat with a fatty liquid, the fat rises. When you
pour, the stock comes out while the fat stays behind
in the jug.

3 **Chilling** This technique works best with stock made
from meat, as the fat solidifies when cold. Put the
stock in the refrigerator until the fat becomes solid,
then remove the pieces of fat using a slotted spoon.

Making soups

Soups are nutritious, full of flavour and easy to make. Incredibly versatile, they can be smooth or chunky, light for a first course or substantial for a main course, made with vegetables, pulses, meat, chicken or fish.

Puréeing soups

1 **Using a jug blender** Allow the soup to cool slightly, then fill the jug about half-full, making sure that there is more liquid than solids. Cover the lid with a teatowel and hold it on tightly. Blend until smooth, then add more solids and blend again until all the soup is smooth. (If you have a lot of soup, transfer each batch to a clean pan.)

2 **Using a stick blender** Allow the soup to cool slightly. Stick the blender deep into the soup, switch it on, and move it about so that all the soup is puréed. **Note:** don't do this in a non-stick pan.

3 **Using a mouli** A mouli-légumes makes a fine purée, although it takes longer than using a blender. Fit the fine plate to the mouli-légumes and set it over a bowl – put a teatowel underneath to keep it from moving on the table. Fill the bowl of the mouli about halfway up the sides, putting in more solids than liquid. Work in batches if you have a large quantity of soup.

4 **Using a sieve** If you don't have a blender or mouli-légumes, you can purée soup by pushing it through a sieve, although this will take a much longer time.

Partially puréed soups

1 For an interesting texture, purée one-third to half of the ingredients, then stir back into the soup.

2 Alternatively, prepare the vegetables or other ingredients, but set aside a few choice pieces. While the soup is cooking, steam or boil these pieces until just tender; refresh green vegetables in cold water. Just before serving, cut into smaller pieces and add to the soup.

Chunky soups

1 Cut the ingredients into bite-size pieces. Heat oil or butter in the soup pan and cook the onions – and garlic if you like – until soft and lightly coloured.

2 Add the remaining ingredients, putting in those that need the longest cooking first. Pour in some stock and bring to the boil.

3 Simmer gently until all the ingredients are tender. If too much liquid boils away, just add more.

Simple Vegetable Soup

You can use almost any mixture of vegetables.
To serve four, you will need:
1 or 2 finely chopped onions, 2 tbsp oil or 1 tbsp oil and 25g (1oz) butter, 1 or 2 crushed garlic cloves (optional), 450g (1lb) chopped mixed vegetables, such as leeks, potatoes, celery, fennel, canned tomatoes and parsnips (chopped finely or cut into larger dice for a chunky soup), 1.1 litres (2 pints) stock.

1 Fry the onions in the oil or oil and butter until soft, and add the garlic if you like.

2 Add the chopped mixed vegetables and the stock. Bring to the boil and simmer for 20–30 minutes until the vegetables are tender.

3 Leave chunky, partially purée or blend until smooth.

Trimming meat

Trim away excess fat, leaving no more than 5mm (¼in) on steaks, chops and roasting cuts - a little fat will contribute juiciness and flavour. When preparing meat for cutting into chunks, try to seperate the individual muscles, which can be identified by the sinews running between each muscle.

Preparing and cooking meat

Beef, lamb, pork, ham and game such as rabbit and venison make wonderfully hearty one-pot meals, and are easy to prepare and cook when you know how. For perfectly cooked meat, choose the appropriate method for the cut. Tender cuts need quick cooking, such as grilling, whereas tougher cuts benefit from slower cooking, such as pot-roasting.

Marinades

Meat is good for marinating, either wet or dry, because its large surface area allows maximum exposure to the marinade. Marinate small pieces of meat for at least 8 hours, and thick joints for 24 hours.

Wet marinades

These almost always contain some form of acid, which has a modest tenderising effect (especially in thin cuts such as steak). Before cooking, dry marinated meat thoroughly to remove liquid from the surface, and cook the marinade (skimming off the oil if necessary) as a sauce or deglazing liquid.

Good additions to wet marinades:
Onions and shallots, chopped or sliced
Asian spices, such as Chinese five-spice powder and star anise
Chilli
Sherry or sherry vinegar
Brandy

Dry marinades

These are useful for roasts and pot roasts. They don't penetrate far into the meat, but give an excellent flavour on and just under the crust. Make them with crushed garlic, dried herbs or spices, and plenty of freshly ground black pepper. Rub into the meat and marinate for at least 30 minutes or up to 8 hours.

Stir-frying

Perfect for tender cuts of meat.

1 Trim the fat, then cut the meat into strips or dice no thicker than 5mm (¼in).

2 Heat a wok or large pan until hot and add oil to coat the inside. Add the meat and cook, stirring. Set aside. Cook the other ingredients you are using (such as vegetables and flavourings). Return the meat to the wok for 1–2 minutes to heat through.

Braising and pot-roasting

Tougher cuts of meat (see box below right) require slow cooking. Braises and pot roasts are similar, but braises need more liquid.

To serve six, you will need:
3 tbsp olive oil, 1.1kg (2½lb) meat, cut into large chunks, or 6 lamb shanks, 1 large onion, 3 carrots, 3 celery sticks, all thickly sliced, 2 garlic cloves, crushed, 2 x 400g cans chopped tomatoes, 150ml (¼ pint) white wine, salt and ground black pepper, 2 bay leaves.

1 Preheat the oven to 170°C (150°C fan oven) mark 3. Heat the oil in a large flameproof casserole and lightly brown the meat all over, in two or three batches. Remove from the pan; set aside. Add the onion, carrots, celery and garlic and cook until beginning to colour, then add the meat, tomatoes and wine.

2 Stir well, season and add the bay leaves. Bring to the boil, cover, and transfer to the oven for 2 hours or until tender. Skim off fat if necessary.

Perfect braising and pot-roasting

- Good cuts of beef include shin, chuck, blade, brisket and flank; good cuts of lamb include leg, shoulder, neck, breast and shank; good cuts of pork include shoulder, hand, spring, belly and loin.
- Cuts you would normally roast can also be casseroled. These simply need less time in the oven.
- Always use a low heat, and check regularly to make sure that there is enough liquid to keep the meat from catching on the casserole.
- Braises often improve by being cooked in advance and then gently reheated before serving. If you've braised a whole piece of meat, you can slice it before reheating.

Preparing and cooking poultry

From the simplest, healthiest stir-frying, steaming and poaching to the more robust pot-roasting and casseroling, there are numerous ways to make the most of the delicate taste of poultry.

Jointing

You can buy pieces of chicken in a supermarket or from a butcher, but it is more economical to joint a whole bird yourself. Use the wing tips and bones to make stock (see page 11).

1 Using a sharp meat knife with a curved blade, cut out the wishbone and remove the wings in a single piece. Remove the wing tips.

2 With the tail pointing towards you and breast side up, pull one leg away and cut through the skin between leg and breast. Pull the leg down until you crack the joint between the thigh bone and ribcage. Cut through that joint, then cut through the remaining leg meat. Repeat on the other side.

3 To remove the breast without any bone, make a cut along the length of the breastbone. Gently teasing the flesh away from the ribs with the knife, work the blade down between the flesh and ribs of one breast and cut it off neatly. (Always cut in, towards the bone.) Repeat on the other side.

4 To remove the breast with the bone in, make a cut along the full length of the breastbone. Using poultry shears, cut through the breastbone, then cut through the ribcage following the outline of the breast meat. Repeat on the other side. Trim off any flaps of skin or fat.

Pot-roasting

To serve four to six, you will need:
2 tbsp vegetable oil, 1 onion, cut into wedges, 2 rashers rindless streaky bacon, chopped, 1.4–1.6kg (3–3½lb) chicken, 2 small turnips, cut into wedges, 6 carrots, halved, 1 garlic clove, crushed, bouquet garni, 600ml (1 pint) chicken stock, 100ml (3½fl oz) dry white wine, small handful of parsley, chopped, salt and pepper.

1 Preheat the oven to 200°C (180°C fan oven) mark 6. Heat the oil in a flameproof casserole. Fry the onion and bacon for 5 minutes. Set aside. Add the chicken, brown all over for 10 minutes, then set aside. Fry the turnips, carrots and garlic for 2 minutes, then add the bacon, onion and chicken.

2 Add the bouquet garni, stock, wine and season. Bring to the boil and transfer to the oven. Cook, basting now and then, for 1 hour 20 minutes or until the juices run clear. Lift out the chicken, stir parsley into liquid and carve the chicken.

Casseroling

To serve four to six, you will need:
1 chicken, jointed, 3 tbsp oil, 1 onion, chopped, 2 garlic cloves, crushed, 2 celery sticks, chopped, 2 carrots, chopped, 1 tbsp plain flour, 2 tbsp chopped tarragon or thyme, chicken stock and/or wine, salt and pepper.

1 Preheat the oven to 180°C (160°C fan oven) mark 4. Cut the chicken legs and breasts in half.

2 Heat the oil in a flameproof casserole and brown the chicken all over. Remove and pour off the excess oil. Add the onion and garlic and brown for a few minutes. Add the vegetables, then stir in the flour and cook for 1 minute. Add the herbs and season. Add the chicken and pour in stock and/or wine to come three-quarters of the way up the poultry. Cook for 1–1½ hours.

Poaching

This gentle method of cooking will produce a light broth.

1 Brown the bird in oil if you like (this is not necessary but will give a deeper flavour), then transfer to a pan that will hold it easily: a large frying pan or sauté pan is good for pieces, a flameproof casserole for a whole bird.

2 Add 1 roughly chopped onion, 2 crushed garlic cloves, 2 chopped carrots, 2 chopped celery sticks, 6 whole black peppercorns and 1 tsp dried mixed herbs. Pour in just enough stock to cover, then simmer, uncovered, for 30–40 minutes (for pieces) or about 1 hour (for a whole bird).

3 Gently lift the bird out of the liquid. If you are planning to use the liquid as the basis for a sauce, reduce it by at least half.

Perfect pot-roasted poultry

- Pot-roasting is the perfect way to cook almost any poultry or game bird apart from duck or goose, which are too fatty and do not give good results, and turkey, which is too large to fit in the average casserole dish.
- Make sure that you use a large enough casserole and that the bird isn't too close to the sides of the dish.
- Check the liquid level in the casserole from time to time. If it's too dry, add a little more. Water is fine; stock or wine is even better.
- Timings for pot-roasted poultry: about 45 minutes (for small birds such as poussin) or 1–1½ hours (for chicken or guinea fowl).

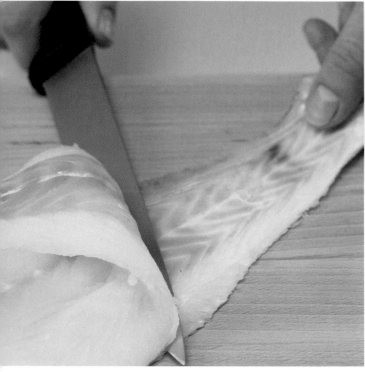

Braising

This is a good method when you want a hearty fish dish.

To serve four, you will need:
1 tbsp oil, 15g (½oz) butter, 1 onion, chopped, 2 garlic cloves, crushed, 2 tbsp each freshly chopped parsley and thyme, 400g can chopped tomatoes, about 900g (2lb) firm-fleshed fish (see box below).

1 Put the oil and butter in a large frying pan and cook the onion and garlic until soft. Add the herbs and tomatoes to the pan, and cook until the tomatoes are fairly thick.

2 Put the fish on the vegetables and spoon the tomatoes over it.

3 Cook for another 5–10 minutes until the fish is just cooked through.

Buying and cooking fish and shellfish

Fish is wonderfully versatile and can be cooked in many ways – from quick pan-frying, grilling and stir-frying and steaming to poaching and braising.

Perfect braised fish

- Choose thick, fairly firm-fleshed fish if you are cooking it in pieces – cod, haddock, monkfish, hake and whiting are all good choices. Shellfish, squid and cuttlefish are also suitable.
- You can choose a variety of vegetables and herbs to use in braised dishes: try adding chopped red pepper and using oregano instead of thyme. Make sure that all the other ingredients are cooked and their flavours well developed before you add the fish.
- Once you add the fish to the pan, don't move it about too much as the flesh can easily break up. Be careful when removing it from the pan.

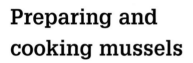

Preparing and cooking mussels

Mussels take moments to cook. Careful preparation is important, so give yourself enough time to get the shellfish ready.

1 Scrape off the fibres attached to the shells (beards). If the mussels are very clean, give them a quick rinse under the cold tap. If they are very sandy, scrub them with a stiff brush.

2 If the shells have sizeable barnacles on them, it's best (though not essential) to remove them. Rap them sharply with a metal spoon or the back of a washing-up brush, then scrape off.

3 Discard any open mussels that don't shut when tapped sharply; this means they are dead and could be dangerous to eat.

4 In a large, heavy-based pan, fry 2 finely chopped shallots and a generous handful of parsley in 25g (1oz) butter for about 2 minutes until soft. Pour in 1cm (½in) dry white wine.

5 Add the mussels to the pan and cover tightly with a lid. Steam for 5–10 minutes until the shells open. Immediately take the pan away from the heat.

6 Using a slotted spoon, remove the mussels from the pan and discard any that haven't opened, then boil the cooking liquid rapidly to reduce. Pour over the mussels and serve immediately.

How to buy the best fish and shellfish

Fish should be as fresh as possible. It's often hard to tell how fresh a piece of fish is, but a really fresh fish has some key signs to look for.
- An even covering of scales with no patches and no damage to the fins.
- Bright and clear eyes and bright red gills.
- Flesh that feels firm rather than soft and spongy.
- Individual fillets should be moist, shiny and plump.

When buying fresh molluscs such as mussels or clams, choose those with tightly closed, undamaged shells.

An open shell may indicate that the shellfish is not fresh; tap the shell - it should close; if it doesn't, discard it.

Preparing vegetables

The following frequently used vegetables can be quickly prepared to add flavour to savoury dishes. Onions and shallots have a pungent taste that becomes milder when they are cooked, and they are often used as a basic flavouring. Tomatoes and peppers add depth and richness to a variety of dishes. Garlic and chillies are stronger flavouring ingredients.

Onions

1 Cut off the tip and base of the onion. Peel away all the layers of papery skin and any discoloured layers underneath.

2 Put the onion root end down on the chopping board, then, using a sharp knife, cut the onion in half from tip to base.

3 **Slicing** Put one half on the board, with the cut surface facing down, and slice across the onion.

4 **Chopping** Slice the halved onions from the root end to the top at regular intervals. Next, make two or three horizontal slices through the onion, then slice vertically across the width.

Seeding peppers

1 Cut the pepper in half vertically and snap out the white pithy core and seeds. Trim away the rest of the white membrane with a knife.

2 Alternatively, slice off the top of the pepper, then cut away and discard the seeds and white pith.

Garlic

1 Put the clove on a chopping board and place the flat side of a large knife on top of it. Press down firmly on the flat of the blade to crush the clove and break the papery skin.

2 Cut off the base of the clove and slip the garlic out of its skin.

3 **Slicing** Using a rocking motion with the knife tip on the board, slice the garlic as thinly as you need.

4 **Shredding and chopping** Holding the slices together, shred them across the slices. Chop the shreds if you need chopped garlic.

5 **Crushing** After step 2, either use a garlic press or crush with a knife: roughly chop the peeled cloves and put them on the board with a pinch of salt. Press down hard with the edge of a large knife tip (with the blade facing away from you), then drag the blade along the garlic while still pressing hard. Continue to do this, dragging the knife tip over the garlic to make a purée.

Seeding unpeeled tomatoes

1 Halve the tomato through the core. Use a small sharp knife or a spoon to remove the seeds and juice. Shake off the excess liquid.

2 Chop the tomato as required for the recipe and place in a colander for a minute or two to drain off any excess liquid.

Chillies

1 Cut off the cap and slit open lengthways. Using a spoon, scrape out the seeds and the pith.

2 For diced chilli, cut into thin shreds lengthways, then cut crossways.

Cook's Tip

Wash hands thoroughly after handling chillies – the volatile oils will sting if accidentally rubbed into your eyes.

Stir-frying

Stir-frying is perfect for non-starchy vegetables, as the quick cooking preserves their colour, freshness and texture.

To serve four, you will need:
450g (1lb) vegetables, 1–2 tbsp vegetable oil, 2 garlic cloves, crushed, 2 tbsp soy sauce, 2 tsp sesame oil.

1 Cut the vegetables into even-sized pieces. Heat the oil in a large wok or frying pan until smoking-hot. Add the garlic and cook for a few seconds, then remove and set aside.

2 Add the vegetables to the wok, and toss and stir them. Keep them moving constantly as they cook, which will take 4–5 minutes.

3 When the vegetables are just tender, but still with a slight bite, turn off the heat. Put the garlic back into the wok and stir well. Add the soy sauce and sesame oil, toss and serve.

Cooking vegetables

Nutritious, mouthwatering and essential to a healthy diet – vegetables are ideal for adding to one-pot dishes.

Perfect stir-frying

- Cut everything into small pieces of uniform size so that they cook quickly and evenly.
- If you're cooking onions or garlic with the vegetables, don't keep them over a high heat for too long or they will burn.
- Add liquids towards the end of cooking, so they don't evaporate.

Stewing

1 Cut the vegetables into large, bite-size pieces, no more than about 5cm (2in) square. Put them into a heatproof casserole (for oven cooking) or a heavy-based pan (for hob cooking). Add salt and pepper and flavourings if you like (see Perfect stews box below), and mix well.

2 Preheat the oven to 180°C (160°C fan oven) mark 4 if you are cooking in the oven.

3 Pour in stock to come about three-quarters of the way up the vegetables. Cover the dish with a lid or foil and cook for 30–40 minutes until the vegetables are tender but not disintegrating.

4 Turn the vegetables once during cooking, and baste with the juices a few times.

Braising

1 Prepare the vegetables (see Perfect Braising box below right). Pack tightly in an ovenproof dish. Preheat the oven to 180°C (160°C fan oven) mark 4. Dot generously with butter and season with salt.

2 Pour in stock to come halfway up the vegetables. Cover and bake for 30–40 minutes until the vegetables are soft. Baste them with the buttery stock a few times during cooking.

Perfect stews

- Any vegetable can be stewed; be careful not to overcook it.
- Ideal flavourings for stewed vegetables include garlic, shallots, curry powder (or Indian spices), and chilli sauce or chopped chilli.
- Potatoes will thicken the dish a little as they release some of their starch.

Perfect braising

- Carrots, fennel, leeks, celeriac, celery and cabbage are good braised.
- Leave vegetables whole or cut into chunks. Shred cabbage, then fry lightly before braising.
- Cook the vegetables in a single layer.

Eggs

Eggs are a wonderfully versatile ingredient that can be enjoyed on their own – cooked simply – or used in literally hundreds of different ways.

Baking

You can crack eggs into individual dishes or into a large, shallow dish and bake them. They may be cooked on their own, or baked with meat or vegetable accompaniments.

1 Generously smear individual baking dish(es) or one large baking dish with butter.

2 Put in any accompaniments, if using (see Variations and accompaniments below). If using a vegetable-based accompaniment, use the back of a spoon to make a hollow or hollows in which to break the egg or eggs. Carefully crack the egg or eggs into the hollows.

3 Bake for 8–10 minutes at 200°C (180°C fan oven) mark 6, or 15–18 minutes at 180°C (160°C fan oven) mark 4, until the whites are just set; the yolks should still be quite runny.

Variations and Accompaniments

- Eggs are delicious baked on a simple bed of sautéed vegetables (such as ratatouille), lightly browned diced potatoes with onions, and well-cooked spinach.
- Accompaniments must be fully cooked before they are transferred to the baking dish and the raw eggs put on top.
- Begin with a layer of hot-smoked salmon, roughly flaked, and snipped fresh chives.
- If you like, drizzle a small spoonful of cream and a good grinding of black pepper on top of the eggs before baking.
- Other simple additions include chopped fresh herbs or a few shreds of crisp bacon.

Potato and Chorizo Tortilla

To serve four, you will need:
6 tbsp olive oil, 450g (1lb) potatoes, very thinly sliced, 225g (8oz) onions, thinly sliced, 2 garlic cloves, chopped, 50g (2oz) chorizo, cut into strips, 6 large eggs, salt and ground black pepper.

1 Heat the oil in an 18cm (7in) non-stick frying pan. Add the potatoes, onion and garlic, and stir to coat. Cover. Cook gently for 15 minutes, stirring occasionally, until the potato is soft. Season with salt.

2 Add the chorizo to the pan. Beat the eggs and season with salt and pepper, then pour into the pan and cook for about 5 minutes until the edges are beginning to brown and the egg looks about three-quarters set.

3 Put the tortilla under a preheated grill and quickly brown the top. Remove from the heat and leave to cool. Loosen the edges and serve cut into wedges.

Making omelettes

There are numerous different types of omelette – from the classic folded omelette made from simple beaten eggs to thick omelettes such as Spanish tortilla and Italian frittata.

Classic Omelette

To serve one, you will need: 15g (½oz) butter, 2 eggs, beaten, salt and ground black pepper.

1 Add the butter to a preheated heavy-based 18cm (7in) frying pan and let it sizzle for a few moments without browning, then pour in the beaten eggs and stir a few times with a fork.

2 As the omelette begins to stick at the sides of the pan, lift it up and let the uncooked egg run into the gap.

3 When the omelette is nearly set and the underneath is brown, loosen the edges and give the pan a sharp shake to slide the omelette across.

4 Add a filling (such as grated cheese or fried mushrooms) if you like, and fold the far side of the omelette towards you. Tilt the pan to slide the omelette on to the plate and serve.

Perfect omelettes

- Beat the eggs lightly.
- Use a high heat.
- Don't add butter until the pan is already hot, otherwise it will become overbrown.

Fruit

Most fruits taste marvellous raw, although a few always need to be cooked. Nearly all fruits make superb desserts when they are baked, poached or stewed.

Classic Poached Pears

To serve four, you will need:
300g (11oz) sugar, 4 ripe pears, juice of 1 lemon.

1 Put the sugar in a large measuring jug and fill with cold water to make 1 litre (1½ pints). Transfer to a pan and heat gently, stirring now and then, until the sugar has dissolved.

2 Peel and halve the pears, and toss gently with lemon juice.

3 Pour the sugar syrup in a wide-based pan and bring to a simmer. Put in the pears, cut sides down. They should be completely covered with syrup: add a little more syrup if necessary.

4 Simmer the fruit very gently for 30–40 minutes until the pears are soft when pierced with a knife. Serve hot, warm or cold.

Baking

The key to success when baking fruit is in keeping the cooking time short, so that the delicate flesh of the fruit doesn't break down completely. Preheat the oven to 200°C (180°C fan oven) mark 6.

1 Prepare the fruit and put in a single layer in a buttered baking dish or individual dishes. Put a splash of water in the bottom of the dish(es). (For extra flavour, you can use fruit juice or wine instead of water, if you prefer.) Sprinkle with sugar (and other flavourings such as spices, citrus zest or vanilla, if you like). Dot with butter.

2 Bake the fruit until just tender when pierced with a knife or skewer: this should take 15–25 minutes depending on the fruit and the size of the pieces. Leave to rest for a few minutes before serving.

Stewing

To serve four, you will need:
450g (1lb) prepared fruit (chunks of apples and rhubarb, whole gooseberries, halved plums), sugar to taste, 1 tbsp lemon juice.

1 Put the fruit in a non-stick stainless-steel pan with the sugar. Add the lemon juice and 2 tbsp water. Bring to the boil over a medium heat, then turn down the heat and simmer gently, partly covered, until the fruit is soft, stirring often.

Good fruits for baking

Fruit	Preparation
Apples (dessert or cooking)	Cored and halved or quartered
Apricots	Whole or halved and stoned
Bananas	Peeled and halved, or in their skins
Berries	Whole
Nectarines and peaches	Halved and stoned
Pears	Cored and halved or quartered
Pineapple	Cored and cut into large chunks
Plums	Whole or halved and stoned

Zesting citrus fruits

Citrus zest is an important flavouring and is simple to prepare.

1 Wash and thoroughly dry the fruit. Using a vegetable peeler or small sharp knife, cut away the zest (the coloured outer layer of skin), taking care to leave behind the bitter white pith. Continue until you have removed as much as you need.

2 Stack the slices of zest on a board and shred or dice as required using a sharp knife.

Easy zesting

- To use a zester, press the blade into the citrus skin and run it along the surface to take off long shreds.
- To use a grater, rub the fruit over the grater, using a medium pressure to remove the zest without taking off the white pith as well.

Food storage and hygiene

Storing food properly and preparing it in a hygienic way is important in order to ensure that food remains as nutritious and flavourful as possible, and to reduce the risk of food poisoning.

Hygiene

When you are preparing food, always follow these important guidelines:

Wash your hands thoroughly before handling food and again between handling different types of food, such as raw and cooked meat and poultry. If you have any cuts or grazes on your hands, be sure to keep them covered with a waterproof plaster.

Wash down worksurfaces regularly with a mild detergent solution or multi-surface cleaner.

Use a dishwasher if available. Otherwise, wear rubber gloves for doing the washing-up, so that the water temperature can be hotter than unprotected hands can bear. Change drying-up cloths and cleaning cloths regularly. Note that leaving dishes to drain is more hygienic than drying them with a teatowel.

Keep raw and cooked foods separate, especially meat, fish and poultry. Wash kitchen utensils in between preparing raw and cooked foods. Never put cooked or ready-to-eat foods on a surface that has just had raw fish, meat or poultry on it.

Keep pets out of the kitchen if possible; or make sure they stay away from worksurfaces. Never allow animals on worksurfaces.

Shopping

Always choose fresh ingredients in prime condition, and go to stores and markets that have a regular turnover of stock to ensure freshness of the produce.

Make sure items are within their 'best before' or 'use by' date. (Foods with a long shelf life have a 'best before' date; more perishable items have a 'use by' date.)

Pack frozen and chilled items in an insulated cool bag at the check-out and put them into the freezer or refrigerator as soon as you get home.

During warm weather in particular, buy perishable foods just before you return home. When packing items at the check-out, sort them according to where you will store them when you get home – the refrigerator, freezer, storecupboard, vegetable rack, fruit bowl, etc. This will make unpacking easier – and quicker.

The storecupboard

Although storecupboard ingredients generally last a long time, correct storage is important:

Always check packaging for storage advice – even with familiar foods, because storage requirements may change if additives, sugar or salt have been reduced.

Check storecupboard foods for their 'best before' or 'use by' date and do not use them if the date has passed.

Keep all food cupboards scrupulously clean and make sure food containers and packets are properly sealed.

Once opened, treat canned foods as though fresh. Always transfer the contents to a clean container, cover and keep in the refrigerator. Similarly, jars, sauce bottles and cartons should be kept chilled after opening. (Check the label for storage time after opening.)

Transfer dry goods such as sugar, rice and pasta to moisture-proof containers. When supplies are used up, wash the container well and dry thoroughly before refilling with new supplies.

Store oils in a dark cupboard away from any heat source as heat and light can make them turn rancid and affect their colour. For the same reason, buy olive oil in dark green bottles.

Store vinegars in a cool place; they can turn bad in a warm environment.

Store dried herbs, spices and flavourings in a cool, dark cupboard or in dark jars. Buy in small quantities as their flavour will not last indefinitely.

Store flours and sugars in airtight containers.

Refrigerator storage

Fresh food needs to be kept in the cool temperature of a refrigerator to keep it in good condition and discourage the growth of harmful bacteria. Store day-to-day perishable items, such as opened jams and jellies, mayonnaise and bottled sauces, in the refrigerator along with eggs and dairy products, fruit juices, bacon, fresh and cooked meat (on separate shelves), and salads and vegetables (except potatoes, which don't suit being stored in the cold). A refrigerator should be kept at an operating temperature of 4–5°C. It is worth investing in a refrigerator thermometer to ensure the correct temperature is maintained.

To ensure your refrigerator is functioning effectively for safe food storage, follow these guidelines:

To avoid bacterial cross-contamination, store cooked and raw foods on separate shelves, putting cooked foods on the top shelf. Ensure that all items are well wrapped.

Never put hot food into the refrigerator, as this will cause the internal temperature of the refrigerator to rise.

Avoid overfilling the refrigerator, as this restricts the circulation of air and prevents the appliance from working properly.

It can take some time for the refrigerator to return to the correct operating temperature once the door has been opened, so don't leave it open any longer than is necessary.

Clean the refrigerator regularly, using a specially formulated germicidal refrigerator cleaner. Alternatively, use a weak solution of bicarbonate of soda: 1 tbsp to 1 litre (1¾ pints) water.

If your refrigerator doesn't have an automatic defrost facility, defrost regularly.

Maximum refrigerator storage times

For pre-packed foods, always adhere to the 'use by' date on the packet. For other foods the following storage times should apply, providing the food is in prime condition when it goes into the refrigerator and that your refrigerator is in good working order:

Vegetables and Fruit

Green vegetables	3–4 days
Salad leaves	2–3 days
Hard and stone fruit	3–7 days
Soft fruit	1–2 days

Dairy Food

Cheese, hard	1 week
Cheese, soft	2–3 days
Eggs	1 week
Milk	4–5 days

Fish

Fish	1 day
Shellfish	1 day

Raw Meat

Bacon	7 days
Game	2 days
Joints	3 days
Minced meat	1 day
Offal	1 day
Poultry	2 days
Raw sliced meat	2 days
Sausages	3 days

Cooked Meat

Joints	3 days
Casseroles/stews	2 days
Pies	2 days
Sliced meat	2 days
Ham	2 days
Ham, vacuum-packed (or according to the instructions on the packet)	1–2 weeks

Soups

Cook's Tip

Once you have added the eggs, don't boil the soup or the eggs will curdle.

Herb and Lemon Soup

1.7 litres (3 pints) chicken stock

150g (5oz) orzo or other dried soup pasta

3 medium eggs

juice of 1 large lemon

2 tbsp finely chopped fresh chives

2 tbsp finely chopped fresh chervil

salt and ground black pepper

lemon wedges to serve

1 Bring the stock to the boil in a large pan. Add the pasta and cook for 5 minutes or according to the packet instructions.

2 Beat the eggs in a bowl until frothy, then add the lemon juice and 1 tbsp cold water. Slowly stir in two ladlefuls of the hot stock. Put the egg mixture in the pan with the rest of the soup, then warm through over a very low heat for 2–3 minutes.

3 Add the chives and chervil, and season with salt and pepper. Divide the soup among six warmed bowls and serve immediately, with lemon wedges.

Serves 6	EASY		NUTRITIONAL INFORMATION	
	Preparation Time 10 minutes	**Cooking Time** 15 minutes	**Per Serving** 130 calories, 4g fat (of which 1g saturates), 18g carbohydrate, 1.8g salt	Dairy free

Roasted Tomato and Pepper Soup

1.4kg (3lb) full-flavoured tomatoes, preferably vine-ripened

2 red peppers, cored, seeded and chopped

4 garlic cloves, crushed

3 small onions, thinly sliced

20g (³⁄₄oz) fresh thyme sprigs

4 tbsp olive oil

4 tbsp Worcestershire sauce

4 tbsp vodka

salt and ground black pepper

6 tbsp double cream to serve

1 Preheat the oven to 200°C (180°C fan oven) mark 6. Put the tomatoes in a large roasting tin with the peppers, garlic and onions. Scatter 6 thyme sprigs over the top, drizzle with olive oil and roast in the oven for 25 minutes. Turn the vegetables over and roast for a further 30–40 minutes until tender and slightly charred.

2 Put one-third of the vegetables into a blender or food processor with 300ml (½ pint) boiled water. Add the Worcestershire sauce and vodka, and season with salt and pepper. Whiz until smooth, then pass through a sieve into a pan.

3 Whiz the remaining vegetables with 450ml (³⁄₄ pint) boiled water, then sieve and add to the pan.

4 To serve, warm the soup thoroughly, stirring occasionally. Pour into warmed bowls, add 1 tbsp double cream to each bowl, then drag a cocktail stick through the cream to swirl. Scatter a few fresh thyme leaves over the top, and serve immediately.

EASY		NUTRITIONAL INFORMATION		Serves
Preparation Time 20 minutes	**Cooking Time** about 1 hour	**Per Serving** 239 calories, 16g fat (of which 6g saturates), 15g carbohydrate, 0.4g salt	Gluten free	**6**

Summer Vegetable Soup with Herb Pistou

3 tbsp sunflower oil

1 onion, finely chopped

225g (8oz) waxy potatoes, finely diced

175g (6oz) carrots, finely diced

1 medium turnip, finely diced

4 bay leaves

6 large fresh sage leaves

2 courgettes, about 375g (13oz), finely diced

175g (6oz) green beans, trimmed and halved

125g (4oz) shelled small peas

225g (8oz) tomatoes, seeded and finely diced

1 small broccoli head, broken into florets

salt and ground black pepper

Pistou (see Cook's Tip) or ready-made pesto to serve

1 Heat the oil in a large pan over a gentle heat. Add the onion, potato, carrot and turnip, and cook for 10 minutes. Pour in 1.7 litres (3 pints) cold water, season with salt and pepper, bring to the boil and add the bay and sage leaves. Simmer for 25 minutes.

2 Add the courgettes, beans, peas and tomatoes. Bring back to the boil and simmer for 10–15 minutes. Add the broccoli 5 minutes before the end of the cooking time.

3 Remove the bay and sage leaves and adjust the seasoning. Pour the soup into warmed bowls and serve immediately; serve the pistou or pesto separately to stir into the hot soup.

Cook's Tip

Pistou is a Provençal condiment similar to Italian pesto. To make your own, using a pestle and mortar or a small bowl and the end of a rolling pin, or a mini processor, pound together $3/4$ tsp sea salt and 6 garlic cloves, chopped, until smooth. Add 15g ($1/2$oz) fresh basil, chopped, and pound to a paste, then mix in 12 tbsp olive oil, a little at a time. Store in a sealed jar in the refrigerator for up to one week.

Serves 6	EASY		NUTRITIONAL INFORMATION	
	Preparation Time 20 minutes	**Cooking Time** 1 hour	**Per Serving** 163 calories, 7g fat (of which 1g saturates), 17g carbohydrate, 0.1g salt	Vegetarian Gluten free • Dairy free

Leek and Potato Soup

25g (1oz) butter
1 onion, finely chopped
1 garlic clove, crushed
550g (1¼lb) leeks, chopped
200g (7oz) floury potatoes, peeled and sliced
1.3 litres (2¼ pints) hot vegetable stock
crème fraîche and chopped chives to garnish

1 Melt the butter in a pan over a gentle heat, and cook the onion for 10–15 minutes until soft. Add the garlic and cook for a further 1 minute. Add the leeks and cook for 5–10 minutes until softened. Add the potatoes and toss together with the leeks.

2 Pour in the hot stock and bring to the boil. Simmer the soup for 20 minutes until the potatoes are tender. Cool a little, then purée in a food processor.

3 Reheat before serving, garnished with crème fraîche and chives.

Serves 4	EASY		NUTRITIONAL INFORMATION	
	Preparation Time 10 minutes	**Cooking Time** 45 minutes	**Per Serving** 117 calories, 6g fat (of which 4g saturates), 13g carbohydrate, 0.1g salt	Vegetarian

Freezing Tip

To freeze Complete the recipe, cool and put in a freezerproof container. Seal and freeze for up to three months.
To use Thaw for 4 hours at cool room temperature. Put in a pan, bring to the boil and simmer for 10 minutes.

Sweet Potato Soup

1 tbsp olive oil

1 large onion, finely chopped

2 tsp coriander seeds, crushed

2 fresh red chillies, seeded and chopped (see page 41)

1 butternut squash, about 750g (1lb 10oz), peeled and roughly chopped

2 sweet potatoes, peeled and roughly chopped

2 tomatoes, skinned and diced

1.7 litres (3 pints) hot vegetable stock

cheese straws to serve

1 Heat the oil in a large pan over a gentle heat and fry the onion for about 10 minutes until soft. Add the coriander seeds and chillies to the pan and cook for 1–2 minutes.

2 Add the squash, sweet potatoes and tomatoes, and cook for 5 minutes. Add the hot stock, cover and bring to the boil. Simmer gently for 15 minutes or until the vegetables are soft. Using a blender, whiz the soup in batches until smooth. Reheat gently and serve with cheese straws.

EASY		NUTRITIONAL INFORMATION		Serves
Preparation Time 20 minutes	**Cooking Time** 35 minutes	**Per Serving** 78 calories, 2g fat (of which trace saturates), 14g carbohydrate, 0.8g salt	Vegetarian Dairy free	**8**

Freezing Tip

To freeze Complete the recipe to the end of step 2, then cool, pack and freeze for up to one month.
To use Thaw the soup overnight at cool room temperature, then complete the recipe.

40g (1½oz) butter

1 onion, roughly chopped

225g (8oz) floury potatoes such as King Edward, peeled and chopped

400g (14oz) parsnips, peeled and chopped

4 tsp paprika, plus extra to dust

1.1 litres (2 pints) vegetable stock

450ml (¾ pint) milk

4 tbsp double cream

75g (3oz) sliced chorizo sausage, cut into fine strips

salt and ground black pepper

parsnip crisps and freshly grated Parmesan to serve

Parsnip Soup with Chorizo

1 Melt the butter in a large heavy-based pan over a gentle heat. Add the onion and cook for 5 minutes until soft. Add the potatoes, parsnips and paprika. Mix well and cook gently, stirring occasionally, for 15 minutes or until the vegetables begin to soften.

2 Add the stock, milk and cream, and season with salt and pepper. Bring to the boil and simmer for about 25 minutes or until the vegetables are very soft. Add 50g (2oz) of the chorizo. Allow the soup to cool a little, then whiz in a blender or food processor until smooth. The soup can be thinned with additional stock or milk, if you like. Check the seasoning and put back in the pan.

3 To serve, reheat the soup. Serve in warmed bowls and top each with parsnip crisps; sprinkle with the remaining chorizo and a little Parmesan and dust with paprika.

Serves	EASY		NUTRITIONAL INFORMATION
8	**Preparation Time** 20 minutes	**Cooking Time** 1 hour	**Per Serving** 278 calories, 20g fat (of which 9g saturates), 18g carbohydrate, 0.7g salt

Smoked Cod and Sweetcorn Chowder

130g pack cubed pancetta

50g (2oz) butter

3 leeks, about 450g (1lb), trimmed and thinly sliced

25g (1oz) plain flour

600ml (1 pint) semi-skimmed or full-fat milk

700g (1½lb) undyed smoked cod loin or haddock, skinned and cut into 2cm (¾in) cubes

326g can sweetcorn in water, drained

450g (1lb) small new potatoes, sliced

150ml (¼ pint) double cream

½ tsp paprika

salt and ground black pepper

2 tbsp freshly chopped flat-leafed parsley to garnish

1 Fry the pancetta in a large pan over a gentle heat until the fat runs out. Add the butter to the pan to melt, then add the leeks and cook until softened.

2 Stir in the flour and cook for a few seconds, then pour in the milk and 300ml (½ pint) cold water. Add the fish to the pan with the sweetcorn and potato. Bring to the boil and simmer for 10–15 minutes until the potatoes are cooked.

3 Stir in the cream, season with salt and pepper and the paprika, and cook for 2–3 minutes to warm through. Ladle into warmed shallow bowls and sprinkle each one with a little chopped parsley. Serve immediately.

EASY		NUTRITIONAL INFORMATION	Serves
Preparation Time 5 minutes	**Cooking Time** 20 minutes	**Per Serving** 517 calories, 28g fat (of which 15g saturates), 35g carbohydrate, 4.7g salt	**6**

Cook's Tip

This is really two meals in one, a starter and a main course. The beef flavours the stock and is removed before serving. Later you divide up the meat and serve it with mashed potatoes, swedes or turnips.

Scotch Broth

1 piece of marrow bone, about 350g (12oz)

1.4kg (3lb) piece of beef skirt (ask your butcher for this)

300ml (½ pint) broth mix (to include pearl barley, red lentils, split peas and green peas), soaked according to the packet instructions

2 carrots, finely chopped

1 parsnip, finely chopped

2 onions, finely chopped

¼ white cabbage, finely chopped

1 leek, finely chopped

1–2 tbsp salt

ground black pepper

2 tbsp freshly chopped parsley to serve

1 Put the marrow bone and beef skirt into a 5.7 litre (10 pint) stock pot and add 2.6 litres (4½ pints) cold water – there should be enough to cover the meat.

2 Bring the water to the boil. Remove any scum from the surface with a spoon and discard. Reduce the heat to low, add the broth mix and simmer, partially covered, for 1½ hours, skimming the surface occasionally.

3 Add the carrots, parsnip, onions, cabbage, leek and another 600ml (1 pint) cold water. Cover to bring to the boil quickly, then simmer for 30 minutes.

4 Remove the marrow bone and piece of beef from the broth. Add a few shreds of beef to the broth if you like. Season the broth well with the salt and some pepper, stir in the chopped parsley and serve hot.

Serves 8	EASY		NUTRITIONAL INFORMATION	
	Preparation Time 15 minutes	**Cooking Time** 2 hours	**Per Serving** 173 calories, 2g fat (of which trace saturates), 35g carbohydrate, 2.3g salt	Dairy free

Cook's Tips

Chillies vary enormously in strength, from quite mild to blisteringly hot, depending on the type of chilli and its ripeness. Taste a small piece first to check it's not too hot for you. To prepare, see page 21.

Be extremely careful when handling chillies not to touch or rub your eyes with your fingers, as they will sting. Wash knives immediately after handling chillies for the same reason. As a precaution, use rubber gloves when preparing them if you like.

1 tbsp olive oil

4 boneless skinless chicken thighs, around 300g (11oz), shredded

3 garlic cloves, roughly chopped

2 red chillies, seeded and finely diced (see Cook's Tip)

1 lemongrass stalk, finely sliced

5cm (2in) piece of fresh root ginger, finely chopped

150ml (¼ pint) white wine

1 litre (1¾ pints) chicken stock

8 fresh coriander sprigs

50g (2oz) rice noodles

125g (4oz) green beans, trimmed and halved

125g (4oz) bean sprouts

4 spring onions, finely sliced

2 tbsp Thai fish sauce (nam pla)

juice of ½ lime

salt and ground black pepper

Thai Chicken Broth

1 Heat the oil in a large pan over a medium heat. Add the chicken, garlic, chillies, lemongrass and ginger, and cook for 3–5 minutes until the chicken is opaque.

2 Add the wine, bring to the boil and simmer until reduced by half. Add the stock and bring to the boil. Simmer for 5 minutes or until the chicken is cooked through.

3 Pick the leaves off the coriander and put them to one side. Finely chop the coriander stalks. Add the noodles to the pan and cook for 1 minute, then add the beans and coriander stalks. Cook for 3 minutes.

4 Add the bean sprouts and spring onions (reserving a few to garnish) along with the fish sauce and lime juice. Bring to the boil and taste for seasoning. Ladle the noodles and broth into four warmed bowls, making sure that each serving has some chicken and bean sprouts. Garnish with the coriander leaves, spring onions and bean sprouts and serve.

EASY		NUTRITIONAL INFORMATION		Serves
Preparation Time 20 minutes	**Cooking Time** 20–25 minutes	**Per Serving** 198 calories, 5g fat (of which 1g saturates), 13g carbohydrate, 1.1g salt	Dairy free	4

Spiced Beef and Noodle Soup

2 tbsp sunflower oil

225g (8oz) fillet steak, cut into thin strips

1.1 litres (2 pints) beef stock

2–3 tbsp Thai fish sauce (nam pla)

1 large red chilli, seeded and finely sliced (see page 41)

1 lemongrass stalk, trimmed and thinly sliced

2.5cm (1in) piece of root ginger, finely shredded

6 spring onions, halved lengthways and cut into 2.5cm (1in) lengths

1 garlic clove, crushed

¼ tsp caster sugar

15g (½oz) dried porcini or shiitake mushrooms, broken into pieces and soaked in 150ml (¼ pint) boiling water for 15 minutes

50g (2oz) medium egg noodles

125g (4oz) spinach leaves, roughly chopped

4 tbsp freshly chopped coriander

salt and ground black pepper

1 Heat the oil in a large pan, then brown the meat in two batches and put to one side.

2 Pour the stock into the pan with 2 tbsp of the fish sauce, the chilli, lemongrass, ginger, spring onions, garlic and sugar. Add the mushrooms and their soaking liquid. Bring the mixture to the boil.

3 Break up the noodles slightly and add them to the pan, then stir gently until they begin to separate. Simmer the soup, stirring occasionally, for 4–5 minutes until the noodles are just tender.

4 Stir in the spinach, coriander and reserved beef. Season with salt and pepper, adding the remaining fish sauce to taste, then serve the soup in warmed bowls.

EASY		NUTRITIONAL INFORMATION		Serves
Preparation Time 20 minutes	Cooking Time 15 minutes	Per Serving 215 calories, 13g fat (of which 3g saturates), 11g carbohydrate, 1.2g salt	Dairy free	4

2

Easy Suppers

Try Something Different

Instead of courgettes use leftover boiled potatoes, cut into small cubes.

Courgette and Parmesan Frittata

40g (1½oz) butter

1 small onion, finely sliced

225g (8oz) courgettes, finely sliced

6 medium eggs, beaten

25g (1oz) freshly grated Parmesan, plus shavings to garnish

salt and ground black pepper

crusty bread to serve

1 Melt 25g (1oz) of the butter in an 18cm (7in) non-stick frying pan, and cook the onion until soft. Add the courgettes and fry gently for 5 minutes or until they begin to soften.

2 Preheat the grill. Add the remaining butter to the frying pan. Season the eggs with salt and pepper, and pour into the pan. Cook for 2–3 minutes until golden underneath and cooked around the edges.

3 Scatter the grated cheese over the frittata and put under the preheated grill for 1–2 minutes or until just set. Garnish with Parmesan shavings, cut the frittata into quarters and serve with crusty bread.

Serves 4	EASY		NUTRITIONAL INFORMATION	
	Preparation Time 10 minutes	**Cooking Time** 15 minutes	**Per Serving** 457 calories, 38g fat (of which 18g saturates), 5g carbohydrate, 1.2g salt	Gluten free

2kg (4½lb) fresh mussels, scrubbed, rinsed and beards removed (see page 19)

25g (1oz) butter

4 shallots, finely chopped

2 garlic cloves, crushed

200ml (7fl oz) dry white wine

2 tbsp freshly chopped flat-leafed parsley

100ml (3½fl oz) single cream

salt and ground black pepper

crusty bread to serve

Moules Marinière

1 Tap the mussels on the worksurface, and discard any that do not close or have broken shells. Heat the butter in a large non-stick lidded frying pan, and sauté the shallots over a medium-high heat for about 10 minutes until soft.

2 Add the garlic, wine and half the parsley to the pan, and bring to the boil. Tip in the mussels and reduce the heat a little. Cover and cook for about 5 minutes or until all the shells have opened; discard any mussels that don't open.

3 Lift out the mussels with a slotted spoon and put into serving bowls, and cover with foil to keep warm. Add the cream to the stock, season with salt and pepper, and cook for 1–2 minutes to heat through.

4 Pour a little sauce over the mussels and sprinkle with the rest of the parsley. Serve immediately with crusty bread.

EASY		NUTRITIONAL INFORMATION		Serves
Preparation Time 15 minutes	**Cooking Time** 20 minutes	**Per Serving** 266 calories, 13g fat (of which 7g saturates), 2g carbohydrate, 0.9g salt	Gluten free	**4**

Try Something Different

Instead of prawns use skinless chicken breast, cut into thin strips.

Prawns in Yellow Bean Sauce

250g pack medium egg noodles

1 tbsp stir-fry oil or sesame oil

1 garlic clove, sliced

1 tsp freshly grated ginger

1 bunch of spring onions, trimmed and each stem cut into four lengthways

250g (9oz) frozen raw peeled tiger prawns, thawed

200g (7oz) pak choi, leaves separated and the white base cut into thick slices

160g jar Chinese yellow bean stir-fry sauce

1 Put the noodles in a bowl, pour 2 litres (3½ pints) boiling water over them and leave to soak for 4 minutes. Drain and set aside.

2 Heat the oil in a wok over a medium heat. Add the garlic and ginger and stir-fry for 30 seconds. Add the spring onions and prawns, and cook for 2 minutes.

3 Add the chopped white part of the pak choi and the yellow bean sauce. Fill the empty sauce jar with boiling water and pour this into the wok, too.

4 Add the noodles to the pan and continue to cook for 1 minute, tossing every now and then to heat through. Finally, stir in the green pak choi leaves and serve immediately.

Serves 4	EASY		NUTRITIONAL INFORMATION	
	Preparation Time 10 minutes, plus 4 minutes standing	**Cooking Time** 5 minutes	**Per Serving** 394 calories, 10g fat (of which 2g saturates), 59g carbohydrate, 0.9g salt	Dairy free

Navarin of Cod

175g (6oz) podded broad beans

25g (1oz) butter

2 tbsp sunflower oil

1 onion, sliced

225g (8oz) baby carrots, trimmed and halved

225g (8oz) courgettes, cut into 2cm (³/₄in) chunks

1 garlic clove, crushed

1.1kg (2¹/₂lb) thick cod fillet, skinned

4 tbsp plain flour

150ml (¹/₄ pint) dry white wine

300ml (¹/₂ pint) fish stock

1 tbsp lemon juice

3 tbsp double cream

2 tbsp freshly chopped flat-leafed parsley

salt and ground black pepper

baby new potatoes to serve (optional)

1 If the beans are large, blanch them in boiling water for 1–2 minutes, then drain and refresh in cold water.

2 Heat half the butter and half the oil in a large sauté pan. Add the onion, carrots, courgettes and garlic, and cook gently until softened and just beginning to brown. Remove from the pan and put to one side.

3 Season the fish with salt and pepper, then dust lightly with the flour. Heat the remaining butter and oil in the pan, add the fish and brown on all sides. Remove from the pan and put to one side.

4 Add the wine to the pan, scraping up any sediment from the bottom. Simmer for 1–2 minutes, then put the carrot mixture and fish back in the pan. Add the beans and stock. Bring to a simmer, cover and simmer gently for about 10 minutes until the fish is opaque and flakes easily. Stir in the lemon juice, cream and parsley. Divide among six bowls and serve with baby new potatoes, if you like.

EASY		NUTRITIONAL INFORMATION	Serves
Preparation Time 15 minutes	**Cooking Time** 25 minutes	**Per Serving** 346 calories, 13g fat (of which 5g saturates), 16g carbohydrate, 0.4g salt	**6**

Chilli Vegetable and Coconut Stir-fry

2 tbsp sesame oil

2 green chillies, seeded and finely chopped (see page 41)

2.5cm (1in) piece of fresh root ginger, finely grated

2 garlic cloves, crushed

1 tbsp Thai green curry paste

125g (4oz) carrot, cut into fine matchsticks

125g (4oz) baby sweetcorn, halved

125g (4oz) mangetouts, halved on the diagonal

2 large red peppers, finely sliced

2 small pak choi, quartered

4 spring onions, finely chopped

300ml (½ pint) coconut milk

2 tbsp peanut satay sauce

2 tbsp light soy sauce

1 tsp soft brown sugar

4 tbsp freshly chopped coriander, plus extra sprigs to garnish

ground black pepper

roasted peanuts to garnish

rice or noodles to serve

1 Heat the oil in a wok or large non-stick frying pan over a medium heat, and stir-fry the chillies, ginger and garlic for 1 minute. Add the curry paste and fry for a further 30 seconds.

2 Add the carrot, sweetcorn, mangetouts and red peppers. Stir-fry over a high heat for 3–4 minutes, then add the pak choi and spring onions. Cook, stirring, for a further 1–2 minutes.

3 Pour in the coconut milk, satay sauce, soy sauce and sugar. Season with pepper, bring to the boil and cook for 1–2 minutes, then add the chopped coriander. Garnish with the peanuts and coriander sprigs, and serve with rice or noodles.

Serves 4	EASY		NUTRITIONAL INFORMATION	
	Preparation Time 25 minutes	Cooking Time about 10 minutes	Per Serving 220 calories, 12g fat (of which 2g saturates), 22g carbohydrate, 1.7g salt	Vegetarian Dairy free

▼ Spanish Chicken Parcels
▶ Oranges with Caramel Sauce
   (see page 118)

Spanish Chicken Parcels

12 boneless, skinless chicken thighs, around 900g (2lb)

180g jar pimientos or roasted red peppers, drained

12 thin slices chorizo sausage

2 tbsp olive oil

1 onion, finely chopped

4 garlic cloves, crushed

225g can chopped tomatoes

4 tbsp dry sherry

18 Queen green olives

salt and ground black pepper

rice or crusty bread to serve

1 Put the chicken thighs on a board, season well with salt and pepper and put a piece of pimiento inside each one. Wrap a slice of chorizo around the outside and secure with two cocktail sticks. Put to one side.

2 Heat the olive oil in a pan over a medium heat, and fry the onion for 10 minutes. Add the garlic and cook for 1 minute. Put the chicken parcels, chorizo-side down, in the pan and brown them all over for 10–15 minutes.

3 Add the chopped tomatoes and sherry to the pan and bring to the boil. Simmer for 5 minutes or until the chicken juices run clear. Add the olives and warm through. Remove the cocktail sticks and serve with rice or crusty bread.

Cook's Tip

Queen green olives are large, meaty olives with a mild flavour.

Serves 6	EASY		NUTRITIONAL INFORMATION	
	Preparation Time 15 minutes	**Cooking Time** about 30 minutes	**Per Serving** 444 calories, 29g fat (of which 9g saturates), 4g carbohydrate, 3.1g salt	Gluten free • Dairy free

▼ **Easy Thai Red Chicken Curry**
▶ **Figs in Cinnamon Syrup (see page 116)**

Easy Thai Red Chicken Curry

1 tbsp vegetable oil

3 tbsp Thai red curry paste

4 skinless chicken breasts, around 600g (1lb 5oz), sliced

400ml can coconut milk

300ml (½ pint) hot chicken or vegetable stock

juice of 1 lime

200g pack mixed baby sweetcorn and mangetouts

2 tbsp freshly chopped coriander

rice or rice noodles to serve

1 Heat the oil in a wok or large pan over a low heat. Add the curry paste and cook for 2 minutes until fragrant.

2 Add the sliced chicken and fry gently for about 10 minutes until browned.

3 Add the coconut milk, stock, lime juice and baby corn to the pan and bring to the boil. Add the mangetouts, reduce the heat and simmer for 4–5 minutes until the chicken is cooked. Add the chopped coriander and serve immediately with rice or noodles.

EASY		NUTRITIONAL INFORMATION		Serves
Preparation Time 5 minutes	**Cooking Time** 20 minutes	**Per Serving** 248 calories, 8g fat (of which 1g saturates), 16g carbohydrate, 1g salt	Dairy free	**4**

Try Something Different

Use pork escalopes cut into thin strips instead
of chicken.

Chicken, Bean and Spinach Curry

1 tbsp sunflower oil
350g (12oz) skinless chicken breasts, cut into strips
1 garlic clove, crushed
300–350g tub or jar curry sauce
400g can aduki beans, drained and rinsed
175g (6oz) ready-to-eat dried apricots
150g (5oz) natural bio yogurt
125g (4oz) ready-to-eat baby spinach
naan bread to serve

1 Heat the oil in a large pan over a medium heat, and fry the chicken strips with the garlic until golden. Add the curry sauce, beans and apricots, then cover and simmer gently for 15 minutes or until the chicken is tender.

2 Over a low heat, stir in the yogurt, keeping the curry hot without boiling it, then stir in the spinach until it just begins to wilt. Serve immediately with naan bread.

Serves 4	EASY		NUTRITIONAL INFORMATION	
	Preparation Time 10 minutes	**Cooking Time** about 20 minutes	**Per Serving** 364 calories, 9g fat (of which 1g saturates), 41g carbohydrate, 2.9g salt	Gluten free

Parma Ham and Artichoke Tagliatelle

500g (1lb 2oz) dried tagliatelle

500ml (18fl oz) crème fraîche

280g jar roasted artichoke hearts, drained and halved

80g pack Parma ham (6 slices), torn into strips

2 tbsp freshly chopped sage leaves, plus extra to garnish

40g (1½oz) Parmesan, pared into shavings with a vegetable peeler

salt and ground black pepper

1 Bring a large pan of water to the boil. Add the pasta, bring back to the boil and cook according to the packet instructions.

2 Drain the pasta well, leaving a ladleful of the cooking water in the pan, then put the pasta back in the pan.

3 Add the crème fraîche, artichokes, Parma ham and chopped sage, and stir everything together. Season well with salt and pepper.

4 Spoon the pasta into warmed bowls, sprinkle over the Parmesan shavings and garnish with sage. Serve immediately.

EASY		NUTRITIONAL INFORMATION	Serves
Preparation Time 5 minutes	**Cooking Time** 10–15 minutes	**Per Serving** 970 calories, 56g fat (of which 36g saturates), 96g carbohydrate, 1g salt	**4**

Cook's Tip

It's important to use spare-rib chops for this recipe, as loin chops won't be tender enough.

Pork Chops with Mustard Sauce

25g (1oz) butter

6 spare-rib pork chops, trimmed of fat (see Cook's Tip)

700g (1½lb) onions, chopped

700g (1½lb) trimmed leeks, chopped

1 garlic clove, crushed

900ml (1½ pints) milk

1 bay leaf

1 fresh thyme sprig

125ml (4fl oz) double cream or crème fraîche

3 tbsp English mustard

salt and ground black pepper

flat noodles, such as tagliatelle, to serve

1 Heat the butter in a flameproof casserole. When the butter is foaming, fry the chops briskly until very light golden brown, then put to one side. Add the onions and leeks, and cook gently until soft; add the garlic and cook for 30 seconds.

2 Pour in the milk and bring to the boil. Put the chops back in the casserole, add the herbs and reduce the heat; bubble gently for 10 minutes. When the pork is tender, transfer to serving plates and keep warm.

3 Bubble the sauce until reduced almost to nothing, then add the cream or crème fraîche and the mustard. Season well with salt and pepper, and pour over the chops. Serve with noodles.

Serves 6	EASY		NUTRITIONAL INFORMATION	
	Preparation Time 15 minutes	**Cooking Time** 30 minutes	**Per Serving** 503 calories, 29g fat (of which 14g saturates), 21g carbohydrate, 1g salt	Gluten free

▼ Pan-fried Chorizo and Potato
▶ Rice Pudding (see page 124)

Pan-fried Chorizo and Potato

2 tbsp olive oil

450g (1lb) potatoes, cut into 2.5cm (1in) cubes

2 red onions, sliced

1 red pepper, seeded and chopped

1 tsp paprika

300g (11oz) piece of chorizo sausage, skinned and cut into chunky slices

250g (9oz) cherry tomatoes

100ml (3½fl oz) dry sherry

2 tbsp freshly chopped flat-leafed parsley

1 Heat the oil in a large heavy-based frying pan over a medium heat. Add the potatoes and fry for 7–10 minutes until lightly browned, turning regularly.

2 Reduce the heat, add the onions and red pepper, and continue to cook for 10 minutes, stirring from time to time, until they have softened but not browned.

3 Add the paprika and chorizo sausage and cook for 5 minutes, stirring from time to time.

4 Add the cherry tomatoes and pour in the sherry. Stir everything together and cook for 5 minutes, until the sherry has reduced and the tomatoes have softened and warmed through.

5 Sprinkle the chopped parsley over the top and serve.

EASY		NUTRITIONAL INFORMATION		Serves
Preparation Time 10 minutes	**Cooking Time** 30 minutes	**Per Serving** 553 calories, 36g fat (of which 12g saturates), 32g carbohydrate, 3.4g salt	Gluten free • Dairy free	**4**

Spicy Sausage and Pasta Supper

1 tbsp olive oil
200g (7oz) salami, sliced
225g (8oz) onion, finely chopped
50g (2oz) celery, finely chopped
2 garlic cloves, crushed
400g can pimientos, drained, rinsed and chopped
400g (14oz) passata or 400g can chopped tomatoes
125g (4oz) sun-dried tomatoes in oil, drained
600ml (1 pint) hot chicken or vegetable stock
300ml (½ pint) red wine
1 tbsp sugar
75g (3oz) dried pasta shapes
400g can borlotti beans, drained and rinsed
salt and ground black pepper
300ml (½ pint) soured cream to serve
175g (6oz) Parmesan, freshly grated, to serve
freshly chopped flat-leafed parsley to garnish

1 Heat the oil in a large pan over a medium heat and fry the salami for 5 minutes or until golden and crisp. Drain on kitchen paper.

2 Fry the onion and celery in the hot oil for 10 minutes or until soft and golden. Add the garlic and fry for 1 minute. Put the salami back in the pan with the pimientos, passata or chopped tomatoes, sun-dried tomatoes, stock, red wine and sugar. Bring to the boil.

3 Stir in the pasta, bring back to the boil and cook for about 10 minutes or according to the packet instructions until the pasta is almost tender.

4 Stir in the beans and simmer for 3–4 minutes. Top up with more stock if the pasta is not tender when the liquid has been absorbed. Season with salt and pepper.

5 Ladle into warmed bowls and serve topped with soured cream and garnished with the chopped parsley. Serve the grated Parmesan separately.

Get Ahead

To prepare ahead Complete the recipe to the end of step 2, cool quickly, cover and chill for up to one day.
To use Bring back to the boil, stir in the pasta and complete the recipe.

EASY		NUTRITIONAL INFORMATION	Serves
Preparation Time 15 minutes	**Cooking Time** 30 minutes	**Per Serving** 629 calories, 39g fat (of which 18g saturates), 36g carbohydrate, 3.1g salt	**6**

Cook's Tip

To make a quick salsa, peel and roughly chop ½ ripe avocado. Put in a bowl with 4 roughly chopped tomatoes, 1 tsp olive oil and the juice of ½ lime. Mix well.

One-pot Spicy Beef

2 tsp sunflower oil

1 large onion, roughly chopped

1 garlic clove, finely chopped

1 small fresh red chilli, finely chopped (see page 41)

2 red peppers, roughly chopped

2 celery sticks, diced

400g (14oz) lean beef mince

400g can chopped tomatoes

2 x 400g cans mixed beans, drained

1–2 tsp Tabasco sauce

2–3 tbsp roughly chopped fresh coriander to garnish (optional)

salsa (see Cook's Tip) and soft flour tortillas or basmati rice to serve

1 Heat the oil in a large heavy-based frying pan over a medium heat. Add the onion to the pan with 2 tbsp water. Cook for 10 minutes or until soft. Add the garlic and chilli, and cook for a further 1–2 minutes until golden. Add the red peppers and celery, and cook for 5 minutes.

2 Add the beef to the pan and brown all over. Add the tomatoes, beans and Tabasco sauce, then simmer for 20 minutes. Garnish with coriander, if you like, and serve with salsa and tortillas or rice.

Serves 4	EASY		NUTRITIONAL INFORMATION	
	Preparation Time 10 minutes	**Cooking Time** 40 minutes	**Per Serving** 487 calories, 21g fat (of which 8g saturates), 45g carbohydrate,1.8g salt	Gluten free • Dairy free

Cook's Tips

You need coarse-textured butcher's sausages for this. The better the sausages, the better the sauce.

To freeze Complete to the end of step 3. Add the pasta and cook for 10 minutes – it will continue to cook right through when you reheat the bolognese. Cool, put in a freezerproof container and freeze for up to three months.

To use Thaw overnight at cool room temperature, put in a pan and add 150ml (¼ pint) water. Bring to the boil, then cover and simmer gently for 10 minutes or until the sauce is hot and the pasta is cooked.

Chunky One-pot Bolognese

3 tbsp olive oil

2 large red onions, finely diced

a few fresh rosemary sprigs

1 large aubergine, finely diced

8 plump coarse sausages

350ml (12fl oz) gutsy red wine

700g (1½lb) passata

4 tbsp sun-dried tomato paste

300ml (½ pint) hot vegetable stock

175g (6oz) small dried pasta such as orecchiette

salt and ground black pepper

1 Heat 2 tbsp of the olive oil in a large, shallow non-stick pan over a low heat. Add the onions and rosemary and cook for 10 minutes or until soft and golden. Add the aubergine and remaining oil and cook over a medium heat for 8–10 minutes until soft and golden.

2 Meanwhile, pull the skin off the sausages and divide each into four rough chunks. Tip the aubergine mixture on to a plate and add the sausage chunks to the hot pan – you won't need any extra oil. Stir the sausage pieces over a high heat for 6–8 minutes until golden and beginning to crisp at the edges.

3 Pour in the wine and leave to bubble for 6–8 minutes until only a little liquid remains. Put the aubergine mixture back in the pan, along with the passata, tomato paste and stock.

4 Stir the pasta into the liquid, cover, then simmer for 20 minutes or until the pasta is cooked. Taste and season if needed.

EASY		NUTRITIONAL INFORMATION		Serves
Preparation Time 10 minutes	**Cooking Time** 55 minutes	**Per Serving** 499 calories, 31g fat (of which 10g saturates), 40g carbohydrate, 1.5g salt	Dairy free	**6**

3

Stews and Casseroles

Cook's Tip

Passata is a useful storecupboard ingredient from the Italian kitchen, which can be used in sauces and stews. It is made from ripe tomatoes that have been puréed and sieved to make a very smooth sauce.

Spanish Fish Stew

350g (12oz) small salad potatoes, halved

175g (6oz) chorizo sausage, skinned and roughly chopped

350g jar roasted peppers in olive oil, drained and chopped, oil reserved

1 garlic clove, crushed

2 small red onions, cut into thick wedges

175ml (6fl oz) dry white wine

300g (11oz) passata

25g (1oz) pitted black olives

450g (1lb) chunky white fish such as cod and haddock, cut into large cubes

salt and ground black pepper

freshly chopped flat-leafed parsley to garnish

1 Preheat the oven to 170°C (150°C fan oven) mark 3. Put the potatoes, chorizo, roasted peppers, garlic, onions, wine and passata into a large flameproof casserole with 2 tbsp of the oil from the peppers. Season with salt and pepper.

2 Bring to the boil over a medium heat, cover with a tight-fitting lid, then cook in the oven for 45 minutes.

3 Add the olives and fish and put back in the oven for 15 minutes or until the fish is opaque and completely cooked through. Spoon into warmed bowls and serve garnished with chopped parsley.

Serves 4	EASY		NUTRITIONAL INFORMATION	
	Preparation Time 20 minutes	**Cooking Time** 1 hour 10 minutes	**Per Serving** 463 calories, 22g fat (of which 6g saturates), 32g carbohydrate,1.8g salt	Gluten free • Dairy free

Cook's Tip

Tom yum paste is a hot and spicy Thai mixture used in soups and stews. It is available from large supermarkets and Asian food shops.

Spicy Monkfish Stew

1 tbsp olive oil

1 onion, finely sliced

1 tbsp tom yum paste (see Cook's Tip)

450g (1lb) potatoes, peeled and cut into 2cm (³⁄₄ in) chunks

400g can chopped tomatoes in rich tomato juice

600ml (1 pint) hot fish stock

450g (1lb) monkfish, cut into 2cm (³⁄₄ in) chunks

200g (7oz) ready-to-eat baby spinach

salt and ground black pepper

1 Heat the oil in a pan over a medium heat and fry the onion for 5 minutes until golden.

2 Add the tom yum paste and potatoes, and stir-fry for 1 minute. Add the tomatoes and hot stock, season well with salt and pepper, and cover. Bring to the boil, then simmer, partially covered, for 15 minutes or until the potatoes are just tender.

3 Add the monkfish to the pan and continue to simmer for 5–10 minutes until the fish is cooked. Add the baby spinach leaves and stir through until wilted.

4 Spoon the fish stew into warmed bowls and serve immediately.

EASY		NUTRITIONAL INFORMATION		Serves
Preparation Time 10 minutes	**Cooking Time** 35 minutes	**Per Serving** 142 calories, 3g fat (of which 1g saturates), 16g carbohydrate, 0.2g salt	Dairy free	**6**

Mussel and Potato Stew

25g (1oz) butter

200g (7oz) rindless back bacon rashers, cut into strips

700g (1½lb) white potatoes, cut into large chunks

200g can sweetcorn, drained

1kg (2¼lb) mussels, scrubbed, rinsed and beards removed (see page 19 and Cook's Tip)

150ml (¼ pint) single cream

1 tbsp freshly chopped flat-leafed parsley

salt and ground black pepper

1 Melt the butter in a large pan, add the bacon and cook, stirring, until the strips separate. Add the potatoes and 150ml (¼ pint) water, and season lightly with salt and pepper. Cover with a tight-fitting lid and cook for 10 minutes or until the potatoes are almost tender.

2 Add the sweetcorn and mussels to the pan, cover, bring to the boil and simmer for 2–3 minutes until the mussels open; discard any mussels that don't open. Add the cream and chopped parsley, and serve immediately.

Cook's Tip

To make sure mussels are safe to eat, check them carefully for cracks and split shells before cooking. Discard these, and any that do not close when tapped sharply. Any mussels that remain closed after cooking should also be thrown away.

EASY		NUTRITIONAL INFORMATION		Serves
Preparation Time 15 minutes	**Cooking Time** 15 minutes	**Per Serving** 470 calories, 23g fat (of which 11g saturates), 42g carbohydrate, 2.8g salt	Gluten free	**4**

Chicken and Vegetable Hotpot

4 chicken breasts, skin on
2 large parsnips, chopped
2 large carrots, chopped
300ml (½ pint) ready-made gravy
125g (4oz) cabbage, shredded
ground black pepper

1 Heat a non-stick frying pan or flameproof casserole until hot. Add the chicken breasts, skin side down, and cook for 5–6 minutes. Turn them over and add the parsnips and carrots. Cook for a further 7–8 minutes.

2 Pour the gravy over the chicken and vegetables, then cover and cook gently for 10 minutes.

3 Season with pepper and stir in the cabbage, then cover and continue to cook for 4–5 minutes until the chicken is cooked through, the cabbage has wilted and the vegetables are tender. Serve hot.

Serves 4	EASY		NUTRITIONAL INFORMATION	
	Preparation Time 5 minutes	**Cooking Time** 30 minutes	**Per Serving** 338 calories, 14g fat (of which 3g saturates), 14g carbohydrate, 1.2g salt	Dairy free

Chicken Tagine with Apricots and Almonds

2 tbsp olive oil
4 chicken thighs
1 onion, chopped
2 tsp ground cinnamon
2 tbsp runny honey
150g (5oz) dried apricots
75g (3oz) blanched almonds
250ml (9fl oz) hot chicken stock
salt and ground black pepper
flaked almonds to garnish
couscous to serve

1 Heat 1 tbsp of the oil in a large flameproof casserole over a medium heat. Add the chicken and fry for 5 minutes until brown. Remove from the casserole and put to one side to keep warm.

2 Add the onion to the pan with the remaining olive oil and fry for 10 minutes until softened.

3 Put the chicken back in the pan with the cinnamon, honey, apricots, almonds and hot chicken stock. Season well, stir once, then cover and bring to the boil. Simmer for 45 minutes or until the chicken is falling off the bone.

4 Garnish with the flaked almonds and serve hot with couscous.

EASY		NUTRITIONAL INFORMATION		Serves
Preparation Time 10 minutes	**Cooking Time** about 1 hour	**Per Serving** 376 calories, 22g fat (of which 4g saturates), 19g carbohydrate, 0.5g salt	Dairy free	**4**

Tarragon Chicken with Fennel

1 tbsp olive oil

4 chicken thighs

1 onion, finely chopped

1 fennel bulb, finely chopped

juice of ½ lemon

200ml (7fl oz) hot chicken stock

200ml (7fl oz) crème fraîche

a small bunch of tarragon, roughly chopped

salt and ground black pepper

1 Preheat the oven to 200°C (180°C fan oven) mark 6. Heat the oil in a large flameproof casserole over a medium to high heat. Add the chicken thighs and fry for 5 minutes or until browned, then remove and put them to one side to keep warm.

2 Add the onion to the pan and fry for 5 minutes, then add the fennel and cook for 5–10 minutes until softened.

3 Add the lemon juice to the pan, followed by the stock. Bring to a simmer and cook until the sauce is reduced by half.

4 Stir in the crème fraîche and put the chicken back in the pan. Stir once to mix, then cover and cook in the oven for 25–30 minutes. Stir the tarragon into the sauce, season with salt and pepper, and serve.

Serves 4	EASY		NUTRITIONAL INFORMATION
	Preparation Time 10 minutes	**Cooking Time** 45–55 minutes	**Per Serving** 334 calories, 26g fat (of which 15g saturates), 3g carbohydrate, 0.5g salt

Variation

Instead of the pheasants, use oven-ready poussins, small corn-fed chickens or small guinea fowl; put an onion wedge inside each bird before browning to impart extra flavour.

Pot-roasted Pheasant with Red Cabbage

25g (1oz) butter
1 tbsp oil
2 oven-ready young pheasants, halved
2 onions, peeled and sliced
450g (1lb) red cabbage, cored and finely shredded
1 tsp cornflour
250ml (8fl oz) red wine
2 tbsp redcurrant jelly
1 tbsp balsamic vinegar
salt and ground black pepper
4 rindless smoked streaky bacon rashers, halved

1 Preheat the oven to 200°C (180°C fan oven) mark 6. Melt the butter with the oil in a large flameproof casserole over a medium to high heat. Add the pheasant halves and brown on all sides, then remove and put to one side. Add the onions and cabbage to the casserole and fry for 5 minutes, stirring frequently, until softened.

2 Blend the cornflour with a little water to make a paste. Add to the casserole with the wine, redcurrant jelly and vinegar. Season with salt and pepper, and bring to the boil, stirring.

3 Arrange the pheasant halves, skin side up, on the cabbage. Put the halved bacon rashers on top. Cover the casserole and cook in the oven for 30 minutes or until the birds are tender (older pheasants would take an extra 10–20 minutes).

4 Serve the pot-roasted pheasants and red cabbage with the cooking juices spooned over them.

EASY		NUTRITIONAL INFORMATION		Serves
Preparation Time 15 minutes	**Cooking Time** about 1 hour	**Per Serving** 659 calories, 21g fat (of which 12g saturates), 11g carbohydrate, 1.4g salt	Gluten free	**4**

Get Ahead

To prepare ahead Cook up to the end of step 3, then cool and chill for up to two days.
To use Bring to the boil and reheat in the oven at 180°C (160°C fan oven) mark 4 for 30–40 minutes.

Cook's Tip

If you can't find guinea fowl, use corn-fed chicken joints instead.

Fruity Guinea Fowl

225g (8oz) onion, roughly chopped
125g (4oz) carrot, roughly chopped
125g (4oz) celery, roughly chopped
6–8 guinea fowl joints, 2kg (4½lb) total weight
750ml (1¼ pints) red wine
1 tsp black peppercorns, crushed
1 tbsp freshly chopped thyme
2 bay leaves
175g (6oz) ready-to-eat dried prunes
3 tbsp vegetable oil
3 garlic cloves, crushed
1 tsp harissa paste
1 tbsp tomato purée
2 tbsp plain flour
300ml (½ pint) chicken stock
225g (8oz) streaky bacon, cut into strips
2 apples, cored and sliced
salt and ground black pepper
mashed potato to serve

1 Put the onion, carrot, celery, guinea fowl, 600ml (1 pint) of the wine, peppercorns, thyme and bay leaves in a large bowl. Cover and marinate for at least 3–4 hours. Soak the prunes in the remaining wine for 3–4 hours.

2 Preheat the oven to 170°C (150°C fan oven) mark 3. Drain and dry the joints (put the vegetables and wine to one side). Heat 2 tbsp of the oil in a large flameproof casserole over a medium heat. Cook the joints in batches until browned on both sides. Remove from the pan and put to one side.

3 Add the marinated vegetables to the same pan (keep the marinade to one side), and stir-fry for 5 minutes. Add the garlic, harissa and tomato purée, and cook for 1 minute. Mix in the flour and cook for 1 minute. Pour in the reserved marinade and stock. Bring to the boil, stirring. Put the joints back in the casserole, with the legs at the bottom. Bring to the boil, season well, cover and cook in the oven for 40 minutes.

4 Heat the remaining oil in a pan, add the bacon and cook, stirring, for 5 minutes or until golden brown. Remove from the pan and put to one side. Cook the apples for 2–3 minutes on each side until golden. Put to one side. Remove the joints from the casserole. Strain the sauce and put back in the pan with the joints. Add the prunes and any juices, the bacon and apples. Heat through in the oven for 10 minutes. Serve with mashed potato.

Serves 6	EASY		NUTRITIONAL INFORMATION	
	Preparation Time 40 minutes, plus 4 hours marinating	**Cooking Time** 1½ hours	**Per Serving** 811 calories, 49g fat (of which 14g saturates), 24g carbohydrate, 1.7g salt	Dairy free

One-pot Gammon

1 tbsp olive oil

1.1kg (2½lb) smoked gammon joint

8 shallots, roughly chopped

3 carrots, cut into chunks

3 celery sticks, cut into chunks

4 large Desirée potatoes, unpeeled and quartered

450ml (15fl oz) apple juice

450ml (15fl oz) hot vegetable stock

½ small Savoy cabbage, shredded

25g (1oz) butter

1 Preheat the oven to 190°C (170°C fan oven) mark 5. Heat the oil in a large flameproof casserole, add the gammon joint and cook, turning once or twice, for 5 minutes until brown all over. Remove from the pan and put to one side.

2 Add the shallots, carrots and celery to the casserole. Fry for 3–4 minutes until starting to soften.

3 Put the gammon back in the casserole with the potatoes, apple juice and stock. Cover and bring to the boil. Transfer to the oven and cook for 50 minutes until the meat is cooked through and the vegetables are tender.

4 Put the casserole back on the hob over a low heat, and stir in the cabbage. Simmer for 2–3 minutes, then stir in the butter and serve immediately.

Serves 4	EASY		NUTRITIONAL INFORMATION
	Preparation Time 15 minutes	**Cooking Time** 1 hour 10 minutes	**Per Serving** 698 calories, 30g fat (of which 11g saturates), 57g carbohydrate, 6.3g salt

Try Something Different

Use chicken joints instead of rabbit.

Rabbit Casserole with Prunes

175g (6oz) ready-to-eat pitted prunes

300ml (½ pint) red wine

3–4 tbsp olive oil

about 2.3kg (5lb) rabbit joints

1 large onion, chopped

2 large garlic cloves, crushed

5 tbsp Armagnac

450ml (¾ pint) light stock

a few fresh thyme sprigs, tied together, or 1 tsp dried thyme, plus extra sprigs to garnish

2 bay leaves

150ml (¼ pint) double cream

125g (4oz) brown-cap mushrooms, sliced

salt and ground black pepper

1 Put the prunes and wine into a bowl. Cover and leave for about 4 hours, then strain, keeping the wine and prunes to one side.

2 Preheat the oven to 170°C (150°C fan oven) mark 3. Heat 3 tbsp oil in a flameproof casserole. Brown the rabbit joints a few at a time, then remove from the casserole. Add the onion and garlic with a little more oil, if needed, and brown lightly. Put the rabbit back in the casserole, add the Armagnac and warm through. Carefully light the Armagnac with a taper or long match, then shake the pan gently until the flames subside.

3 Pour in the stock and the wine from the prunes, and bring to the boil. Add the sprigs of thyme or the dried thyme to the casserole with the bay leaves and plenty of salt and pepper. Cover tightly and cook in the oven for about 1 hour or until tender.

4 Lift the rabbit out of the juices and keep warm. Boil the cooking juices until reduced by half. Add the cream and mushrooms and continue boiling for 2–3 minutes. Stir in the prunes and warm through. Adjust the seasoning, and spoon the sauce over the rabbit to serve. Garnish with sprigs of fresh thyme.

EASY		NUTRITIONAL INFORMATION	Serves
Preparation Time 20 minutes, plus 4 hours soaking	**Cooking Time** 1¼ hours	**Per Serving** 538 calories, 26g fat (of which 13g saturates), 11g carbohydrate, 0.5g salt	**6**

Cook's Tip

To make clarified butter, heat butter in a small pan without allowing it to colour. Skim off the foam; the solids will sink. Pour the clear butter into a bowl through a lined sieve. Leave for 10 minutes. Pour into another bowl, leaving any sediment behind. Cool, then store in a jar in the refrigerator for up to six months.

Lamb, Prune and Almond Tagine

2 tsp coriander seeds

2 tsp cumin seeds

2 tsp chilli powder

1 tbsp paprika

1 tbsp ground turmeric

5 garlic cloves, chopped

6 tbsp olive oil

1.4kg (3lb) lamb leg steaks

75g (3oz) ghee or clarified butter (see Cook's Tip)

2 large onions, finely chopped

1 carrot, roughly chopped

900ml (1½ pints) lamb stock

300g (11oz) ready-to-eat prunes

4 cinnamon sticks

4 bay leaves

50g (2oz) ground almonds

12 shallots

1 tbsp honey

salt and ground black pepper

toasted blanched almonds to garnish

freshly chopped flat-leafed parsley to garnish

couscous to serve

1 Using a pestle and mortar or a blender, combine the coriander, cumin, chilli powder, paprika, turmeric, garlic and 4 tbsp of the oil. Coat the lamb with paste, then cover and chill for at least 5 hours.

2 Preheat the oven to 170°C (150°C fan oven) mark 3. Melt 25g (1oz) of the butter in a large flameproof casserole. Add the onions and carrot, and cook until soft. Remove and put to one side.

3 Fry the paste-coated lamb on both sides in the remaining butter. Add a little of the stock to the casserole and bring to the boil, scraping up the sediment from the bottom. Put the onions and carrot back in the casserole and add 100g (3½oz) of the prunes. Add the remaining stock to the pan with the cinnamon sticks, bay leaves and ground almonds. Season with salt and pepper, cover and cook in the oven for 2 hours or until the meat is really tender.

4 Meanwhile, fry the shallots in the remaining oil and the honey until they turn a deep golden brown. Add to the casserole 30–40 minutes before the end of the cooking time.

5 Take the lamb out of the sauce and put to one side. Bring the sauce to the boil, bubble and reduce to a thick consistency. Put the lamb back in the casserole, add the remaining prunes, then bubble for 3–4 minutes. Garnish with the almonds and parsley, and serve hot with couscous.

EASY		NUTRITIONAL INFORMATION	Serves
Preparation Time 20 minutes, plus minimum 5 hours marinating	**Cooking Time** 2½ hours	**Per Serving** 652 calories, 44g fat (of which 16g saturates), 31g carbohydrate, 0.6g salt	**6**

Cook's Tip

Cooking lamb shanks in a rich sauce in the oven at a low temperature makes the meat meltingly tender.

Braised Lamb Shanks

6 small lamb shanks

450g (1lb) shallots

2 medium aubergines, cut into small dice

2 tbsp olive oil

3 tbsp harissa paste

pared zest of 1 orange and juice of 3 large oranges

200ml (7fl oz) medium sherry

700g (1½lb) passata

300ml (½ pint) hot vegetable or lamb stock

75g (3oz) ready-to-eat dried apricots

75g (3oz) cherries (optional)

large pinch of saffron

couscous and French beans (optional) to serve

1 Preheat the oven to 170°C (150°C fan oven) mark 3. Heat a large flameproof casserole over a medium heat, and brown the lamb shanks all over. Allow

10–12 minutes to do this – the better the colour now, the better the flavour of the finished dish.

2 Remove the lamb and put to one side. Add the shallots, aubergines and oil to the casserole and cook over a high heat, stirring from time to time, until the shallots and aubergines are golden and beginning to soften.

3 Reduce the heat and add the lamb and all the other ingredients except the couscous and beans. The liquid should come halfway up the shanks. Bring to the boil, then cover tightly and put in the oven for 2½ hours. Test the lamb with a fork – it should be so tender that it almost falls off the bone.

4 If the cooking liquid looks too thin, remove the lamb to a heated serving plate, then bubble the sauce on the hob until reduced and thickened. Put the lamb back in the casserole. Serve with couscous and French beans, if you like.

Serves 6	EASY		NUTRITIONAL INFORMATION	
	Preparation Time 20–25 minutes	**Cooking Time** 2¾ hours	**Per Serving** 355 calories, 16g fat (of which 6g saturates), 23g carbohydrate, 1.2g salt	Dairy free

50g (2oz) butter

400g (14oz) leeks, trimmed and sliced

1 onion, chopped

1 tbsp olive oil

800g (1lb 12oz) casserole lamb, cubed and tossed with 1 tbsp plain flour

2 garlic cloves, crushed

800g (1lb 12oz) waxy potatoes such as Desirée, peeled and sliced

3 tbsp freshly chopped parsley

1 tsp freshly chopped thyme

600ml (1 pint) lamb stock

150ml (¼ pint) double cream

Lamb and Leek Hotpot

1 Melt half the butter in a 3.5 litre (6¼ pint) flameproof casserole dish over a low heat. Add the leeks and onion, stir to coat, then cover and cook for 10 minutes. Remove and put to one side.

2 Add the oil to the casserole and heat, then brown the meat in batches with the garlic and plenty of salt and pepper. Remove and put to one side.

3 Preheat the oven to 170°C (150°C fan oven) mark 3. Put half the potatoes in a layer over the bottom of the casserole and season with salt and pepper. Add the reserved meat, then spoon the leek mixture on top. Arrange a layer of overlapping potatoes on top of that, sprinkle with the parsley and thyme, then pour in the stock.

4 Bring the casserole to the boil, cover, then cook on a low shelf in the oven for about 1 hour 50 minutes. Remove the lid, dot with the rest of the butter and add the cream. Cook uncovered for 30–40 minutes until the potatoes are golden brown.

EASY		NUTRITIONAL INFORMATION	Serves
Preparation Time 20 minutes	**Cooking Time** 2 hours 50 minutes	**Per Serving** 549 calories, 37g fat (of which 20g saturates), 25g carbohydrate, 0.5g salt	**6**

Freezing Tip

To freeze Complete the recipe to the end of step 4, without the garnish. Put in a freezerproof container, cool and freeze for up to three months.
To use Thaw overnight at cool room temperature. Preheat the oven to 180°C (160°C fan oven) mark 4. Bring to the boil on the hob, cover tightly and reheat in the oven for about 30 minutes or until piping hot.

Braised Beef with Pancetta and Mushrooms

175g (6oz) smoked pancetta or smoked streaky bacon, cubed

2 leeks, thickly sliced

1 tbsp olive oil

450g (1lb) braising steak, cut into 5cm (2in) pieces

1 large onion, finely chopped

2 carrots, thickly sliced

2 parsnips, thickly sliced

1 tbsp plain flour

300ml (½ pint) red wine

1–2 tbsp redcurrant jelly

125g (4oz) chestnut mushrooms, halved

ground black pepper

freshly chopped flat-leafed parsley to garnish

1 Preheat the oven to 170°C (150°C fan oven) mark 3. Fry the pancetta or bacon in a shallow flameproof casserole for 2–3 minutes until golden. Add the leeks and cook for a further 2 minutes or until they are just beginning to colour. Remove with a slotted spoon and put to one side.

2 Heat the oil in the casserole. Fry the beef in batches for 2–3 minutes until golden brown on all sides. Remove and put to one side. Add the onion and fry over a gentle heat for 5 minutes or until golden. Stir in the carrots and parsnips, and fry for 1–2 minutes.

3 Put the beef back in the casserole; stir in the flour to soak up the juices. Gradually add the wine and 300ml (½ pint) water, then stir in the redcurrant jelly. Season with pepper and bring to the boil. Cover with a tight-fitting lid and cook in the oven for 2 hours.

4 Stir in the leeks, pancetta and mushrooms, cover and cook for a further 1 hour or until everything is tender. Serve hot, sprinkled with chopped parsley.

Serves 4	EASY		NUTRITIONAL INFORMATION	
	Preparation Time 20 minutes	**Cooking Time** about 3½ hours	**Per Serving** 524 calories, 25g fat (of which 9g saturates), 27g carbohydrate, 1.6g salt	Dairy free

Freezing Tip

To freeze Complete the recipe to the end of step 3. Cool quickly and put in a freezerproof container. Seal and freeze for up to one month.
To use Thaw overnight at cool room temperature. Preheat the oven to 180°C (160°C fan oven) mark 4. Bring slowly to the boil on the hob, then cover and reheat in the oven for 20–25 minutes. Complete the recipe.

Beef Casserole with Black Olives

6 tbsp oil
1.1kg (2½lb) stewing steak, cut into 4cm (1½in) cubes
350g (12oz) unsmoked streaky bacon rashers, rind removed and sliced into thin strips
450g (1lb) onions, roughly chopped
3 large garlic cloves
2 tbsp tomato purée
125ml (4fl oz) brandy
1 tbsp plain flour
150ml (¼ pint) red wine
300ml (½ pint) beef stock
1 bouquet garni
225g (8oz) flat mushrooms, quartered if large
125g (4oz) black olives
fresh flat-leafed parsley sprigs to garnish (optional)

1 Heat 3 tbsp oil in a large flameproof casserole over a high heat. Brown the steak in batches until dark chestnut brown; remove and keep warm. Add the bacon and fry until golden brown, then put to one side with the beef.

2 Add the remaining oil and cook the onions over a medium heat for 10–15 minutes until golden. Add the garlic, fry for 30 seconds, then add the tomato purée and cook, stirring, for 1–2 minutes. Add the brandy.

3 Preheat the oven to 170°C (150°C fan oven) mark 3. Bring the casserole to the boil and bubble to reduce by half, then add the flour and mix until smooth. Pour in the wine, bring back to the boil and bubble for 1 minute. Put the steak and bacon back in the casserole, then add enough stock to barely cover the meat. Add the bouquet garni. Bring to the boil, then cover, put in the oven and cook for 1¼–1½ hours until the steak is tender. Add the mushrooms and cook for a further 4–5 minutes.

4 Just before serving, remove the bouquet garni and stir in the black olives. Serve hot, garnished with parsley if you like.

EASY		NUTRITIONAL INFORMATION		Serves
Preparation Time 20 minutes	**Cooking Time** 2 hours 10 minutes	**Per Serving** 704 calories, 45g fat (of which 13g saturates), 9g carbohydrate, 3.3g salt	Dairy free	**6**

Peppered Winter Stew

25g (1oz) plain flour

900g (2lb) stewing venison, beef or lamb, cut into 4cm (1½ in) cubes

5 tbsp oil

225g (8oz) button onions or shallots, peeled with root end intact

225g (8oz) onion, finely chopped

4 garlic cloves, crushed

2 tbsp tomato purée

125ml (4fl oz) red wine vinegar

75cl bottle red wine

2 tbsp redcurrant jelly

1 small bunch of fresh thyme, plus extra sprigs to garnish (optional)

4 bay leaves

1 tbsp coarsely ground black pepper

6 cloves

600–900ml (1–1½ pints) beef stock

900g (2lb) mixed root vegetables, such as carrots, parsnips, turnips and celeriac, cut into 4cm (1½in) chunks; carrots cut a little smaller

salt and ground black pepper

1 Preheat the oven to 180°C (160°C fan oven) mark 4. Put the flour into a plastic bag, season with salt and pepper, then toss the meat in it.

2 Heat 3 tbsp of the oil in a large flameproof casserole over a medium heat, and brown the meat well in small batches. Remove and put to one side.

3 Heat the remaining oil and fry the button onions or shallots for 5 minutes or until golden. Add the chopped onion and the garlic and cook, stirring, until soft and golden. Add the tomato purée and cook for a further 2 minutes, then add the vinegar and wine and bring to the boil. Bubble for 10 minutes.

4 Add the redcurrant jelly, thyme, bay leaves, 1 tbsp pepper, cloves and meat to the pan, together with the vegetables and enough stock to barely cover the meat and vegetables. Bring to the boil, cover and cook in the oven for 1¾–2¼ hours until the meat is very tender. Serve hot, garnished with thyme sprigs if you like.

Freezing Tip

To freeze Complete the recipe to the end of step 4, without the garnish. Cool quickly and put in a freezerproof container. Seal and freeze for up to one month.
To use Thaw overnight at cool room temperature. Preheat the oven to 180°C (160°C fan oven) mark 4. Put in a flameproof casserole, and add an extra 150ml (¼ pint) beef stock. Bring to the boil. Cover and reheat for 30 minutes.

Serves 6	EASY		NUTRITIONAL INFORMATION	
	Preparation Time 20 minutes	Cooking Time 2¾ hours	Per Serving 540 calories, 24g fat (of which 7g saturates), 24g carbohydrate, 1.5g salt	Dairy free

Vegetarian Dishes

Mushroom and Bean Hotpot

3 tbsp olive oil

700g (1½lb) chestnut mushrooms, roughly chopped

1 large onion, finely chopped

2 tbsp plain flour

2 tbsp mild curry paste

150ml (¼ pint) dry white wine

400g can chopped tomatoes

2 tbsp sun-dried tomato paste

2 x 400g cans mixed beans, drained and rinsed

3 tbsp mango chutney

3 tbsp roughly chopped fresh coriander and mint

1 Heat the oil in a large pan over a low heat, and fry the mushrooms and onion until the onion is soft and dark golden. Stir in the flour and curry paste, then cook for 1–2 minutes before adding the wine, tomatoes, sun-dried tomato paste and beans.

2 Bring to the boil, then simmer gently for 30 minutes or until most of the liquid has reduced. Stir in the chutney and herbs before serving.

Serves	EASY		NUTRITIONAL INFORMATION	
6	**Preparation Time** 15 minutes	**Cooking Time** 30 minutes	**Per Serving** 280 calories, 10g fat (of which 1g saturates), 34g carbohydrate, 1.3g salt	Vegetarian Dairy free

Try Something Different

Instead of paprika, use 1 tsp each ground cumin and ground coriander. Garnish with freshly chopped coriander.

Spiced Bean and Vegetable Stew

3 tbsp olive oil

2 small onions, sliced

2 garlic cloves, crushed

1 tbsp sweet paprika

1 small dried red chilli, seeded and finely chopped (see page 41)

700g (1½lb) sweet potatoes, peeled and cubed

700g (1½lb) pumpkin, peeled and cut into chunks

125g (4oz) okra, trimmed

500g jar passata

400g can haricot or cannellini beans, drained

salt and ground black pepper

1 Heat the oil in a large heavy-based pan over a very gentle heat. Add the onion and garlic, and cook for 5 minutes.

2 Stir in the paprika and chilli, and cook for 2 minutes, then add the sweet potatoes, pumpkin, okra, passata and 900ml (1½ pints) cold water. Season generously with salt and pepper.

3 Cover the pan, bring to the boil and simmer for 20 minutes until the vegetables are tender. Add the beans, cook for 3 minutes to warm through, then serve.

EASY		NUTRITIONAL INFORMATION		Serves
Preparation Time 15 minutes	**Cooking Time** 35 minutes	**Per Serving** 262 calories, 7g fat (of which 1g saturates), 44g carbohydrate, 1.3g salt	Vegetarian Gluten free • Dairy free	**6**

▼ Mauritian Vegetable Curry
▶ Poached Plums with Port (see page 117)

Mauritian Vegetable Curry

3 tbsp vegetable oil

1 onion, finely sliced

4 garlic cloves, crushed

2.5cm (1in) piece of fresh root ginger, grated

3 level tbsp medium curry powder

6 fresh curry leaves

150g (5oz) potato, peeled and cut into 1cm (½ in) cubes

125g (4oz) aubergine, cut into 2cm (1in) sticks, 5mm (¼ in) wide

150g (5oz) carrots, peeled and cut into 5mm (¼ in) dice

900ml (1½ pints) vegetable stock

pinch of saffron threads

1 tsp salt

ground black pepper

150g (5oz) green beans, trimmed

75g (3oz) frozen peas

3 tbsp chopped fresh coriander to garnish

1 Heat the oil in a large heavy-based pan over a low heat. Add the onion and fry for 5–10 minutes until golden. Add the garlic, ginger, curry powder and curry leaves, and fry for a further minute.

2 Add the potato and aubergine to the pan and fry, stirring, for 2 minutes. Add the carrots, stock, saffron and salt. Season with plenty of pepper. Cover and cook for 10 minutes until the vegetables are almost tender.

3 Add the beans and peas to the pan and cook for a further 4 minutes. Sprinkle with the chopped coriander and serve.

Get Ahead

To prepare ahead Complete the recipe, without the garnish, and chill quickly. Keep in the refrigerator for up to two days.
To use Put in a pan, cover and bring to the boil, then simmer for 10–15 minutes. Complete the recipe.

Serves	EASY		NUTRITIONAL INFORMATION	
4	**Preparation Time** 15 minutes	**Cooking Time** 30 minutes	**Per Serving** 184 calories, 11g fat (of which 1g saturates), 18g carbohydrate, 1.7g salt	Vegetarian Dairy free

Tomato and Butter Bean Stew

2 tbsp olive oil

1 onion, finely sliced

2 garlic cloves, finely chopped

2 large leeks, sliced

2 x 400g cans cherry tomatoes

2 x 400g cans butter beans, drained and rinsed

150ml (¼ pint) hot vegetable stock

1–2 tbsp balsamic vinegar

salt and ground black pepper

1 Preheat the oven to 180°C (160°C fan oven) mark 4. Heat the oil in a flameproof casserole over a medium heat. Add the onion and garlic, and cook for 10 minutes until golden and soft. Add the leeks and cook, covered, for 5 minutes.

2 Add the tomatoes, beans and hot stock, and season well with salt and pepper. Bring to the boil, then cover and cook in the oven for 35–40 minutes until the sauce has thickened. Remove from the oven, stir in the vinegar and spoon into warmed bowls.

Serves 4	EASY		NUTRITIONAL INFORMATION	
	Preparation Time 10 minutes	**Cooking Time** 50–55 minutes	**Per Serving** 286 calories, 8g fat (of which 1g saturates), 41g carbohydrate, 1.8g salt	Vegetarian Dairy free

Cook's Tip

Choose aubergines that are firm, shiny and blemish-free, with a bright green stem.

Aubergine and Lentil Curry

3 tbsp olive oil
2 aubergines, cut into 2.5cm (1in) chunks
1 onion, chopped
2 tbsp mild curry paste
3 x 400g cans chopped tomatoes
200ml (7fl oz) hot vegetable stock
150g (5oz) red lentils, rinsed
100g (3½oz) spinach leaves
25g (1oz) fresh coriander, roughly chopped
2 tbsp fat-free Greek yogurt
rice to serve

1 Heat 2 tbsp of the oil in a large pan over a low heat, and fry the aubergine chunks until golden. Remove from the pan and put to one side.

2 Heat the remaining oil in the same pan, and fry the onion for 8–10 minutes until soft. Add the curry paste and stir-fry for a further 2 minutes.

3 Add the tomatoes, stock, lentils and reserved aubergines to the pan. Bring to the boil, then reduce the heat to a low simmer, half-cover with a lid and simmer for 25 minutes or according to the lentils' packet instructions.

4 At the end of cooking, stir the spinach, coriander and yogurt through the curry. Serve with rice.

EASY		NUTRITIONAL INFORMATION		Serves
Preparation Time 10 minutes	**Cooking Time** 40–45 minutes	**Per Serving** 335 calories, 15g fat (of which 3g saturates), 39g carbohydrate, 0.2g salt	Vegetarian	**4**

Try Something Different

....

Replace half the black-eye beans with red kidney
beans.

Black-eye Bean Chilli

1 tbsp olive oil

1 onion, chopped

3 celery sticks, finely chopped

2 x 400g cans black-eye beans, drained

2 x 400g cans chopped tomatoes

2 or 3 splashes of Tabasco sauce

3 tbsp freshly chopped coriander

warm tortillas and soured cream to serve

1 Heat the olive oil in a heavy-based frying pan over a low heat. Add the onion and celery, and fry for 10 minutes until softened.

2 Add the black-eye beans to the pan with the tomatoes and Tabasco sauce. Bring to the boil, then simmer for 10 minutes.

3 Just before serving, stir in the chopped coriander. Spoon the chilli on to warm tortillas, and serve with a spoonful of soured cream.

Serves 4	EASY		NUTRITIONAL INFORMATION	
	Preparation Time 10 minutes	**Cooking Time** 20 minutes	**Per Serving** 245 calories, 5g fat (of which 1g saturates), 39g carbohydrate, 1.8g salt	Vegetarian

1 red pepper, halved and seeded

1 green pepper, halved and seeded

1 yellow pepper, halved and seeded

2 tbsp olive oil

1 onion, finely sliced

2 garlic cloves, crushed

1 tbsp harissa paste

2 tbsp tomato purée

½ tsp ground cumin

1 aubergine, diced

400g can chickpeas, drained and rinsed

450ml (¾ pint) vegetable stock

4 tbsp roughly chopped fresh flat-leafed parsley, plus a few sprigs to garnish

salt and ground black pepper

Moroccan Chickpea Stew

1 Preheat the grill and lay the peppers, skin side up, on a baking sheet. Grill for around 5 minutes until the skin begins to blister and char. Put the peppers in a plastic bag, seal and put to one side for a few minutes. When cooled a little, peel off the skins and discard, then slice the peppers and put to one side.

2 Heat the oil in a large heavy-based frying pan over a low heat, add the onion and cook for 5–10 minutes until soft. Add the garlic, harissa, tomato purée and cumin, and cook for 2 minutes.

3 Add the peppers to the pan with the aubergine. Stir everything to coat evenly with the spices and cook for 2 minutes. Add the chickpeas and stock, season well with salt and pepper, and bring to the boil. Simmer for 20 minutes.

4 Just before serving, stir the parsley through the chickpea stew. Serve in warmed bowls, garnished with parsley sprigs.

EASY		NUTRITIONAL INFORMATION		Serves
Preparation Time 10 minutes	Cooking Time 40 minutes	Per Serving 232 calories, 9g fat (of which 1g saturates), 29g carbohydrate, 0.6g salt	Vegetarian Dairy free	4

Tofu Noodle Curry

250g (9oz) fresh tofu

2 tbsp light soy sauce

½ red chilli, chopped (see page 41)

5cm (2in) piece fresh root ginger, peeled and grated

1 tbsp olive oil

1 onion, finely sliced

2 tbsp Thai red curry paste

200ml (7fl oz) coconut milk

900ml (1½ pints) hot vegetable stock

200g (7oz) baby sweetcorn, halved lengthways

200g (7oz) fine green beans

250g (9oz) medium rice noodles

salt and ground black pepper

2 spring onions, sliced diagonally, and 2 tbsp freshly chopped coriander to garnish

1 lime, cut into wedges, to serve

1 Drain the tofu, pat it dry and cut it into large cubes. Put the tofu in a shallow dish with the soy sauce, chilli and ginger. Toss to coat, then leave to marinate for 30 minutes.

2 Heat the oil in a large pan over a medium heat, then add the onion and fry for 10 minutes, stirring, until golden. Add the curry paste and cook for 2 minutes.

3 Add the tofu and marinade, coconut milk, stock and sweetcorn, and season with salt and pepper. Bring to the boil, add the green beans, then reduce the heat and simmer for 8–10 minutes.

4 Meanwhile, put the noodles in a large bowl, pour boiling water over them and soak for 30 seconds. Drain the noodles, then stir into the curry. Pour into bowls and garnish with the spring onions and coriander. Serve immediately, with lime wedges.

Cook's Tip

Check the ingredients in the Thai curry paste: some contain shrimp and are therefore not suitable for vegetarians.

EASY		NUTRITIONAL INFORMATION		Serves
Preparation Time 15 minutes, plus marinating	**Cooking Time** about 25 minutes	**Per Serving** 367 calories, 7g fat (of which 1g saturates), 60g carbohydrate, 2g salt	Vegetarian Dairy free	**4**

Cook's Tip

Oil-water spray is far lower in calories than oil alone and, as it sprays on thinly and evenly, you'll use less. Fill one-eighth of a travel-size spray bottle with oil such as sunflower, light olive or vegetable (rapeseed) oil - then top up with water. To use, shake well before spraying.

Lentil Chilli

oil-water spray (see Cook's Tip)

2 red onions, chopped

1½ level tsp each ground coriander and ground cumin

½ level tsp ground paprika

2 garlic cloves, crushed

2 sun-dried tomatoes, chopped

¼ level tsp crushed dried chilli flakes

125ml (4fl oz) red wine

300ml (½ pint) vegetable stock

2 x 400g cans brown or green lentils, drained and rinsed

2 x 400g cans chopped tomatoes

salt and ground black pepper

sugar to taste

plain low-fat yogurt and rice to serve

1 Spray a saucepan with the oil-water spray and cook the onions for 5 minutes until softened. Add the coriander, cumin and paprika. Combine the garlic, sun-dried tomatoes, chilli, wine and stock and add to the pan. Cover and simmer for 5–7 minutes. Uncover and simmer until the onions are very tender and the liquid is almost gone.

2 Stir in the lentils and canned tomatoes and season with salt and pepper. Simmer, uncovered, for 15 minutes until thick. Stir in the sugar to taste. Remove from the heat.

3 Ladle out a quarter of the mixture and whiz in a food processor or blender. Combine the puréed and unpuréed portions. Serve with yogurt and rice.

Serves 6	EASY		NUTRITIONAL INFORMATION	
	Preparation Time 10 minutes	**Cooking Time** 30 minutes	**Per Serving** 191 calories, 2g fat (of which trace saturates), 30g carbohydrate, 0g salt	Vegetarian Dairy free

Try Something Different

Replace half the aubergines with 400g (14oz) courgettes; use a mix of green and red peppers; garnish with fresh basil instead of thyme.

Roasted Ratatouille

400g (14oz) red peppers, seeded and roughly chopped

700g (1½lb) aubergines, stalk removed, cut into chunks

450g (1lb) onions, peeled and cut into wedges

4 or 5 garlic cloves, unpeeled and left whole

150ml (¼ pint) olive oil

1 tsp fennel seeds

200ml (7fl oz) passata

sea salt and ground black pepper

a few fresh thyme sprigs to garnish

1 Preheat the oven to 240°C (220°C fan oven) mark 9. Put the peppers, aubergine, onions, garlic, olive oil and fennel seeds in a roasting tin. Season with sea salt flakes and pepper, and toss together.

2 Transfer to the oven and cook for 30 minutes (tossing frequently during cooking) or until the vegetables are charred and beginning to soften.

3 Stir the passata through the vegetables, and put the roasting tin back in the oven for 50–60 minutes, stirring occasionally. Garnish with the thyme sprigs and serve.

EASY		NUTRITIONAL INFORMATION		Serves
Preparation Time 15 minutes	**Cooking Time** 1½ hours	**Per Serving** 224 calories, 18g fat (of which 3g saturates), 14g carbohydrate, 0g salt	Vegetarian Gluten free • Dairy free	**6**

5
Rice Dishes

Get Ahead

To prepare ahead, fry the aubergine and onion as in step 1. Cover and keep in a cool place for 1½ hours. **To use** Complete the recipe.

Aubergine and Chickpea Pilaf

4–6 tbsp olive oil
275g (10oz) aubergine, roughly chopped
225g (8oz) onions, finely chopped
25g (1oz) butter
½ tsp cumin seeds
175g (6oz) long-grain rice
600ml (1 pint) vegetable or chicken stock
400g can chickpeas, drained and rinsed
225g (8oz) baby spinach leaves
salt and ground black pepper

1 Heat half the olive oil in a large pan or flameproof casserole over a medium heat. Fry the aubergine for 4–5 minutes, in batches, until deep golden brown. Remove from the pan with a slotted spoon and put to one side. Add the remaining oil to the pan, and cook the onions for 5 minutes or until golden and soft.

2 Add the butter, then stir in the cumin seeds and rice. Fry for 1–2 minutes, pour in the stock, season with salt and pepper, and bring to the boil. Reduce the heat, then simmer, uncovered, for 10–12 minutes until most of the liquid has evaporated and the rice is tender.

3 Remove the pan from the heat. Stir in the chickpeas, spinach and reserved aubergine. Cover with a tight-fitting lid and leave to stand for 5 minutes until the spinach has wilted and the chickpeas are heated through. Adjust the seasoning to taste. Fork through the rice grains to separate and make them fluffy before serving.

Serves 4	EASY		NUTRITIONAL INFORMATION	
	Preparation Time 10 minutes	**Cooking Time** 20 minutes, plus 5 minutes standing	**Per Serving** 462 calories, 20g fat (of which 5g saturates), 58g carbohydrate, 0.9g salt	Vegetarian Gluten free

Cook's Tip

If you can't find pumpkin, use butternut squash.

Pumpkin Risotto with Hazelnut Butter

50g (2oz) butter

175g (6oz) onion, finely chopped

900g (2lb) pumpkin, halved, peeled, seeded and cut into small cubes

2 garlic cloves, crushed

225g (8oz) risotto (arborio) rice

600ml (1 pint) hot chicken stock

grated zest of ½ orange

40g (1½ oz) freshly shaved Parmesan

ground black pepper

For the hazelnut butter

50g (2oz) hazelnuts

125g (4oz) softened butter

2 tbsp freshly chopped flat-leafed parsley

1 To make the hazelnut butter, spread the hazelnuts on a baking sheet and toast under a hot grill until golden brown, turning frequently. Put the nuts in a clean teatowel and rub off the skins, then chop finely. Put the nuts, butter and parsley on a piece of non-stick baking parchment. Season with pepper and mix together. Mould into a sausage shape, twist at both ends and chill.

2 To make the risotto, melt the butter in a large pan and fry the onion until soft but not coloured. Add the pumpkin and sauté over a low heat for 5–8 minutes until just beginning to soften. Add the garlic and rice and stir until well mixed. Increase the heat to medium and add the stock a little at a time, allowing the liquid to be absorbed after each addition. This will take about 25 minutes.

3 Stir in the orange zest and Parmesan, and season with salt and pepper. Serve the risotto with a slice of the hazelnut butter melting on top.

EASY		NUTRITIONAL INFORMATION	Serves
Preparation Time 15 minutes	**Cooking Time** 40 minutes	**Per Serving** 706 calories, 50g fat (of which 27g saturates), 51g carbohydrate, 1.1g salt	**4**

Get Ahead

To prepare ahead Complete to the end of step 3. Cover and keep in a cool place for 1½ hours.
To use Complete the recipe.

Saffron Paella

½ tsp saffron threads

900ml–1.1 litres (1½–2 pints) hot chicken stock

5 tbsp olive oil

2 x 70g packs sliced chorizo sausage

6 boneless, skinless chicken thighs, each cut into three pieces

1 large onion, chopped

4 large garlic cloves, crushed

1 tsp paprika

2 red peppers, seeded and sliced

400g can chopped tomatoes in tomato juice

350g (12oz) long-grain rice

200ml (7fl oz) dry sherry

500g pack ready-cooked mussels

200g (7oz) cooked tiger prawns, drained

juice of ½ lemon

salt and ground black pepper

lemon wedges to garnish

fresh flat-leafed parsley sprigs to garnish (optional)

1 Add the saffron to the hot stock and leave to infuse for 30 minutes. Meanwhile, heat half the oil in a large heavy-based frying pan. Add half the chorizo and fry for 3–4 minutes until crisp. Remove with a slotted spoon and drain on kitchen paper. Repeat with the remaining chorizo; put to one side.

2 Heat 1 tbsp oil in the pan, add half of the chicken and cook for 3–5 minutes until pale golden brown. Remove from the pan and put to one side. Cook the remaining chicken and put to one side.

3 Reduce the heat slightly, heat the remaining oil and add the onion. Cook for 5 minutes or until soft. Add the garlic and paprika, and cook for 1 minute. Put the chicken back in the pan, then add the peppers and the tomatoes.

4 Stir the rice into the pan, then add a third of the stock and bring to the boil. Season with salt and pepper, reduce the heat and simmer, uncovered, stirring continuously until most of the liquid has been absorbed.

5 Add the remaining stock, a little at a time, allowing the liquid to become absorbed after each addition (this should take about 25 minutes). Add the sherry and cook for a further 2 minutes.

6 Add the mussels and their juices to the pan with the prawns, lemon juice and reserved chorizo. Cook for 5 minutes to heat through. Adjust the seasoning and garnish with lemon wedges and parsley if you like.

EASY		NUTRITIONAL INFORMATION		Serves
Preparation Time 5 minutes	**Cooking Time** 20 minutes	**Per Serving** 609 calories, 22g fat (of which 6g saturates), 59g carbohydrate, 1.5g salt	Dairy free	**6**

Try Something Different

Instead of salmon, use undyed smoked haddock fillet.

50g (2oz) butter

700g (1½ lb) onions, sliced

2 tsp garam masala

1 garlic clove, crushed

75g (3oz) split green lentils, soaked in 300ml (½ pint) boiling water for 15 minutes, then drained

750ml (1¼ pints) hot vegetable stock

225g (8oz) basmati rice

1 green chilli, seeded and finely chopped (see page 41)

350g (12oz) salmon fillet

salt and ground black pepper

Salmon Kedgeree

1 Melt the butter in a flameproof casserole over a medium heat. Add the onions and cook for 5 minutes or until soft. Remove a third of the onions and put to one side. Increase the heat and cook the remaining onions for 10 minutes to caramelise. Remove and put to one side.

2 Put the first batch of onions back in the casserole, add the garam masala and garlic, and cook, stirring, for 1 minute. Add the drained lentils and stock, cover and cook for 15 minutes. Add the rice and chilli, and season with salt and pepper. Bring to the boil, cover and simmer for 5 minutes.

3 Put the salmon fillet on top of the rice, cover and continue to cook gently for 15 minutes or until the rice is cooked, the stock absorbed and the salmon opaque.

4 Lift off the salmon and divide into flakes. Put it back in the casserole, and fork through the rice. Garnish with the reserved caramelised onion and serve.

Serves 4	EASY		NUTRITIONAL INFORMATION
	Preparation Time 15 minutes, plus 15 minutes soaking	**Cooking Time** 55 minutes	**Per Serving** 490 calories, 15g fat (of which 2g saturates), 62g carbohydrate, 0.1g salt

Cook's Tip

The word pilaf, or pilau, comes from the Persian *pilaw*. The dish originated in the East and consists of rice flavoured with spices, to which vegetables, poultry, meat, fish or shellfish are added.

Prawn and Vegetable Pilau

250g (9oz) long-grain rice
1 broccoli head, broken into florets
150g (5oz) baby sweetcorn, halved
200g (7oz) sugarsnap peas
1 red pepper, sliced into thin strips
400g (14oz) peeled cooked king prawns

For the dressing
1 tbsp sesame oil
5cm (2in) piece of fresh root ginger, grated
juice of 1 lime
1–2 tbsp light soy sauce

1 Put the rice in a large, wide pan – it needs to be really big, as you're cooking the rice and steaming the veg on top, then tossing it all together. Add 600ml (1 pint) boiling water. Cover, bring to the boil, then reduce the heat to low and cook the rice according to the packet instructions.

2 About 10 minutes before the end of the rice cooking time, add the broccoli, corn, sugarsnaps and red pepper. Stir well, then cover and cook until the vegetables and rice are just tender.

3 Meanwhile, put the prawns into a bowl. Add the sesame oil, ginger, lime and soy sauce. Mix the prawns and dressing into the cooked vegetables and rice, and toss through well. Serve immediately.

EASY		NUTRITIONAL INFORMATION		Serves
Preparation Time 10 minutes	**Cooking Time** 15–20 minutes	**Per Serving** 360 calories, 5g fat (of which 1g saturates), 61g carbohydrate, 1.8g salt	Dairy free	**4**

▼ Seafood Gumbo
▶ Peach Brûlée (see page 121)

Seafood Gumbo

125g (4oz) butter
50g (2oz) plain flour
1–2 tbsp Cajun spice
1 onion, chopped
1 green pepper, seeded and chopped
5 spring onions, sliced
1 tbsp freshly chopped flat-leafed parsley
1 garlic clove, crushed
1 beef tomato, chopped
125g (4oz) garlic sausage, finely sliced
75g (3oz) American easy-cook rice
1.1 litres (2 pints) vegetable stock
450g (1lb) okra, sliced
1 bay leaf
1 fresh thyme sprig
2 tsp salt
$\frac{1}{4}$ tsp cayenne pepper
juice of $\frac{1}{2}$ lemon
4 cloves
500g (1$\frac{1}{4}$lb) frozen mixed seafood (containing mussels, squid and prawns), thawed and drained
ground black pepper

1 Heat the butter in a 2.5 litre (4$\frac{1}{4}$–4$\frac{1}{2}$ pint) heavy-based pan over a low heat. Add the flour and Cajun spice, and cook, stirring, for 1–2 minutes until golden brown. Add the onion, green pepper, spring onions, parsley and garlic. Cook for 5 minutes.

2 Add the tomato, garlic sausage and rice to the pan, and stir well to coat. Add the stock, okra, bay leaf, thyme, salt, cayenne pepper, lemon juice and cloves. Season with black pepper. Bring to the boil and simmer, covered, for 12 minutes or until the rice is tender.

3 Add the seafood and cook for 2 minutes to heat through. Serve the gumbo in deep bowls.

Cook's Tip

Gumbo is a traditional stew from the southern states of the USA, containing meat, vegetables and shellfish, and thickened with okra.

Serves 4	EASY		NUTRITIONAL INFORMATION
	Preparation Time 10 minutes	**Cooking Time** 30 minutes	**Per Serving** 559 calories, 23g fat (of which 3g saturates), 58g carbohydrate, 1.2g salt

▼ Caribbean Chicken
▶ Baked Apples (see page 125)

Caribbean Chicken

10 chicken pieces, such as thighs, drumsticks, wings or breasts, skinned

1 tsp salt

1 tbsp ground coriander

2 tsp ground cumin

1 tbsp paprika

pinch of ground nutmeg

1 fresh Scotch bonnet or other hot red chilli, seeded and chopped (see page 41)

1 onion, chopped

5 fresh thyme sprigs

4 garlic cloves, crushed

2 tbsp dark soy sauce

juice of 1 lemon

2 tbsp vegetable oil

2 tbsp light muscovado sugar

350g (12oz) American easy-cook rice

3 tbsp dark rum (optional)

25g (1oz) butter

2 x 300g cans black-eye beans, drained

ground black pepper

a few fresh thyme sprigs to garnish

1 Pierce the chicken pieces with a knife, put in a container and sprinkle with ½ tsp of the salt, some pepper, the coriander, cumin, paprika and nutmeg.

Add the chilli, onion, thyme leaves and garlic, then pour the soy sauce and lemon juice over and stir to combine. Cover and chill for at least 4 hours.

2 Heat a 3.4 litre (6 pint) heavy-based pan over a medium heat for 2 minutes. Add the vegetable oil and muscovado sugar and cook for 3 minutes or until it turns a rich golden caramel colour. (Be careful not to overcook it as the mixture will blacken and taste burnt – so watch it very closely.)

3 Remove the chicken pieces from the marinade and add to the caramel mixture in the hot pan. Cover and cook over a medium heat for 5 minutes, then turn the chicken and cook, covered, for another 5 minutes until evenly browned. Add the onion and any remaining juices from the marinade. Turn again, then cover and cook for 10 minutes.

4 Add the rice, stir to combine with the chicken, then pour in 900ml (1½ pints) cold water. Add the rum, if using, the butter and the remaining ½ tsp salt. Cover with a lid and simmer over a gentle heat, without lifting the lid, for 20 minutes or until the rice is tender and most of the liquid has been absorbed.

5 Add the black-eye beans to the pan and mix well. Cover and cook for 3–5 minutes until the beans are just warmed through and all the liquid has been absorbed, taking care that the rice doesn't stick to the bottom of the pan. Garnish with the thyme sprigs and serve hot.

EASY		NUTRITIONAL INFORMATION	Serves
Preparation Time 40 minutes, plus at least 4 hours marinating	**Cooking Time** 45–50 minutes	**Per Serving** 617 calories, 39g fat (of which 12g saturates), 25g carbohydrate, 2.1g salt	5

Try Something Different

Use turkey or veal escalopes instead of pork.

Pork, Garlic and Basil Risotto

6 thin pork escalopes

150g (5oz) Parma ham (about 6 slices)

about 6 fresh basil leaves

25g (1oz) plain flour

about 75g (3oz) unsalted butter

175g (6oz) onion, finely chopped

2 garlic cloves, crushed

225g (8oz) risotto (arborio) rice

450ml (¾ pint) white wine

450ml (¾ pint) hot chicken stock

3 tbsp pesto sauce

50g (2oz) grated Parmesan

4 tbsp freshly chopped flat-leafed parsley

1 Preheat the oven to 180°C (160°C fan oven) mark 4. If needed, pound the escalopes carefully with a rolling pin until they are wafer-thin. Lay a slice of Parma ham on each escalope and put a basil leaf on top. Fix in place with a wooden cocktail stick. Season and dip in the flour, dusting off any excess.

2 Melt a small knob of the butter in a deep ovenproof pan and quickly fry the escalopes in batches for 2–3 minutes on each side until lightly golden. Melt a little more butter for each batch. You will need about half the butter at this stage. Remove the escalopes and keep warm, covered, in the oven.

3 Melt about another 25g (1oz) of the butter in the pan and fry the onion for about 10 minutes until soft and golden. Add the garlic and rice, and stir well. Add the wine and stock. Bring to the boil, then put in the oven and cook, uncovered, for 20 minutes.

4 Stir the pesto, Parmesan and parsley into the rice. Put the browned escalopes on top of the rice, cover and put the pan back in the oven for a further 5 minutes or until the rice has completely absorbed the liquid and the escalopes are cooked through and piping hot.

Serves 6	EASY		NUTRITIONAL INFORMATION
	Preparation Time 15 minutes	**Cooking Time** 50 minutes	**Per Serving** 431 calories, 18g fat (of which 6g saturates), 28g carbohydrate, 0.7g salt

Cook's Tip

This is a good way to use leftover roast turkey.

50g (2oz) pinenuts

2 tbsp olive oil

2 onions, sliced

2 garlic cloves, crushed

2 tbsp medium curry powder

6 skinless, boneless chicken thighs or 450g (1lb) skinless cooked chicken, cut into strips

350g (12oz) American easy-cook rice

2 tsp salt

pinch of saffron threads

50g (2oz) sultanas

225g (8oz) ripe tomatoes, roughly chopped

Spiced Chicken Pilau

1 Spread the pinenuts over a baking sheet and toast under a hot grill until golden brown, turning them frequently. Put to one side.

2 Heat the oil in a large heavy-based pan over a medium heat. Add the onions and garlic and cook for 5 minutes until soft. Remove half the onion mixture and put to one side.

3 Add the curry powder and cook for 1 minute, then add the chicken and stir. Cook for 10 minutes if the meat is raw, or for 4 minutes if you're using cooked chicken, stirring from time to time until browned.

4 Add the rice to the pan, stir to coat in the oil, then add 900ml (1½ pints) boiling water, the salt and the saffron. Cover and bring to the boil, then reduce the heat to low and cook for 20 minutes or until the rice is tender and most of the liquid has been absorbed. Stir in the reserved onion mixture and the sultanas, tomatoes and pinenuts. Cook for a further 5 minutes to warm through, then serve.

EASY		NUTRITIONAL INFORMATION	Serves
Preparation Time 15 minutes	**Cooking Time** 35–40 minutes	**Per Serving** 649 calories, 18g fat (of which 2g saturates), 87g carbohydrate, 2.8g salt	**4**

Cook's Tip

Jambalaya is a rice-based dish from Louisiana that traditionally contains spicy sausage, chicken, ham or prawns and lots of chilli pepper.

Beef Jambalaya

275g (10oz) fillet steak, cut into thin strips

4 tsp mild chilli powder

1 tsp ground black pepper

about 5 tbsp oil

150g (5oz) chorizo sausage, sliced and cut into strips, or 125g (4oz) cubed

2 celery sticks, cut into 5cm (2in) strips

2 red peppers, cut into 5cm (2in) strips

150g (5oz) onions, roughly chopped

2 garlic cloves, crushed

275g (10oz) long-grain white rice

1 tbsp tomato purée

1 tbsp ground ginger

2 tsp Cajun seasoning

900ml (1½ pints) beef stock

8 large cooked prawns, peeled and deveined

salt

mixed salad to serve

1 Put the steak into a plastic bag with 1 tsp of the chilli powder and the black pepper, seal and shake to mix.

2 Heat 1 tbsp of the oil in a large heavy-based frying pan, and cook the chorizo until golden. Add the celery and red peppers to the pan, and cook for 3–4 minutes until just beginning to soften and brown. Remove from the pan and put to one side. Add 2 tbsp of the oil to the pan, and fry the steak in batches; put to one side and keep warm.

3 Add a little more oil to the pan, if needed, and cook the onion until transparent. Add the garlic, rice, tomato purée, remaining chilli powder, ground ginger and Cajun seasoning, then cook for 2 minutes until the rice turns translucent. Stir in the stock, season with salt and bring to the boil. Cover and simmer for about 20 minutes, stirring occasionally, until the rice is tender and most of the liquid has been absorbed (add a little more water during cooking if needed).

4 Add the reserved steak, chorizo, red peppers and celery, and the prawns. Heat gently, stirring, until piping hot. Adjust the seasoning and serve with a mixed salad.

Serves 4	EASY		NUTRITIONAL INFORMATION	
	Preparation Time 10 minutes	**Cooking Time** 40 minutes	**Per Serving** 554 calories, 30g fat (of which 9g saturates), 40g carbohydrate, 1.8g salt	Dairy free

6

Puddings

Figs in Cinnamon Syrup

1 orange

1 lemon

300ml (½ pint) red wine

50g (2oz) golden caster sugar

1 cinnamon stick

450g (1lb) ready-to-eat dried figs

mascarpone cheese or ice cream to serve

1 Pare the zest from the orange and lemon, and put in a medium pan. Squeeze the orange and lemon and add their juice, the wine, sugar and cinnamon stick to the pan. Bring very slowly to the boil, stirring occasionally.

2 Add the figs. Simmer very gently for 20 minutes until plump and soft. Remove the figs, zest and cinnamon with a slotted spoon, and transfer to a serving bowl.

3 Bring the liquid to the boil once again, and bubble for about 5 minutes until syrupy. Pour over the figs, then cool, cover and chill.

4 If you like, warm the figs in the syrup for 3–4 minutes, then serve with mascarpone cheese or ice cream.

Serves 4	EASY		NUTRITIONAL INFORMATION	
	Preparation Time 15 minutes	**Cooking Time** 35 minutes, plus cooling and chilling	**Per Serving** 336 calories, 2g fat (of which 0g saturates), 68g carbohydrate, 0.2g salt	Vegetarian Gluten free • Dairy free

Poached Plums with Port

75g (3oz) golden caster sugar
2 tbsp port
6 large plums, halved and stoned
1 cinnamon stick
ice cream to serve

1 Put the sugar in a pan with 500ml (18fl oz) water. Heat gently until the sugar dissolves. Bring to the boil and simmer rapidly for 2 minutes without stirring.

2 Stir in the port. Add the plums to the pan with the cinnamon stick, and simmer gently for 5–10 minutes until the fruit is tender but still keeping its shape.

3 Remove the plums and put to one side, discarding the cinnamon. Simmer the syrup until it has reduced by two-thirds. Serve the plums warm or cold, drizzled with syrup and with a scoop of vanilla ice cream alongside, if you like.

EASY		NUTRITIONAL INFORMATION		Serves
Preparation Time 5 minutes	**Cooking Time** 20 minutes	**Per Serving** 97 calories, 0g fat, 23g carbohydrate, 0g salt	Vegetarian Gluten free • Dairy free	**4**

Cook's Tip

Use thick-skinned oranges, such as navel oranges, as they're the easiest to peel.

Oranges with Caramel Sauce

6 oranges

25g (1oz) butter

2 tbsp golden caster sugar

2 tbsp Grand Marnier

2 tbsp marmalade

grated zest and juice of 1 large orange

crème fraîche to serve

1 Preheat the oven to 200°C (180°C fan oven) mark 6. Cut away the peel and pith from the oranges, then put the oranges into a roasting tin just big enough to hold them.

2 Melt the butter in a pan and add the golden caster sugar, Grand Marnier, marmalade, orange zest and juice. Heat gently to dissolve the sugar.

3 Pour the sauce over the oranges, and bake in the oven for 30–40 minutes. Serve with crème fraîche.

Serves 6	EASY		NUTRITIONAL INFORMATION	
	Preparation Time 15 minutes	**Cooking Time** 30–40 minutes	**Per Serving** 139 calories, 4g fat (of which 2g saturates), 24g carbohydrate, 0.1g salt	Vegetarian Gluten free

► Parsnip Soup (see page 38)

► Pot-roasted Pheasant (see page 71)

▼ Pears with Hot Fudge Sauce

Pears with Hot Fudge Sauce

75g (3oz) butter

1 tbsp golden syrup

75g (3oz) light muscovado sugar

4 tbsp evaporated milk or single or double cream

4 ripe pears, cored, sliced and chilled

1 Melt the butter, syrup, sugar and evaporated milk or cream together over a very low heat. Stir thoroughly until all the sugar has dissolved, then bring the fudge mixture to the boil without any further stirring.

2 Put each pear in a serving dish and pour the hot fudge sauce over it. Serve immediately.

EASY		NUTRITIONAL INFORMATION		Serves
Preparation Time 5 minutes	**Cooking Time** 15 minutes	**Per Serving** 301 calories, 16g fat (of which 10g saturates), 40g carbohydrate, 0.4g salt	Vegetarian Gluten free	**4**

▶ **Lamb, Prune and Almond Tagine** (see page 77)
▼ **Clafoutis**

350g (12oz) stoned cherries

3 tbsp Kirsch

1 tbsp golden caster sugar

4 large eggs

100g (3½ oz) caster sugar, plus 1 tbsp extra to dust

25g (1oz) flour

150ml (¼ pint) milk

150ml (¼ pint) single cream

1 tsp vanilla extract

icing sugar to dust

thick cream to serve

Clafoutis

1 Put the stoned cherries in a bowl with the Kirsch and the golden caster sugar. Mix together, cover and set aside for 1 hour.

2 Meanwhile, whisk the eggs with the caster sugar and the flour. Bring the milk and the cream to the boil in a heavy-based pan, and pour on to the egg mixture; whisk until combined. Add the vanilla extract and strain the batter into a bowl; cover and let stand for 30 minutes.

3 Preheat the oven to 180°C (160°C fan oven) mark 4. Lightly butter a 1.7 litre (3 pint) shallow ovenproof dish and dust with the extra caster sugar. Spoon the cherries into the dish, whisk the batter and pour it over the top. Bake in the oven for 50–60 minutes until golden and just set. Dust with icing sugar and serve warm with thick cream.

Serves 6	EASY		NUTRITIONAL INFORMATION	
	Preparation Time 25 minutes	**Cooking Time** 1 hour	**Per Serving** 242 calories, 9g fat (of which 4g saturates), 32g carbohydrate, 0.2g salt	Vegetarian

Try Something Different

Use nectarines instead of peaches.

Peach Brûlée

4 ripe peaches, halved and stone removed

8 tsp soft cream cheese

8 tsp golden caster sugar

1 Preheat the grill until very hot. Fill each stone cavity in the fruit with 2 tsp cream cheese, then sprinkle each one with 2 tsp caster sugar.

2 Put the fruit halves on a grill pan, and cook under the very hot grill until the sugar has browned and caramelised to create a brûlée crust. Serve warm.

EASY		NUTRITIONAL INFORMATION		Serves
Preparation Time 10 minutes	**Cooking Time** about 10 minutes	**Per Serving** 137 calories, 6g fat (of which 4g saturates), 21g carbohydrate, 0.1g salt	Vegetarian Gluten free	**4**

Quick Apple Tart

375g packet all-butter ready-rolled puff pastry

500g (1lb 2oz) Cox's apples, cored, thinly sliced and tossed in the juice of 1 lemon

golden icing sugar to dust

1 Preheat the oven to 200°C (180°C fan oven) mark 6. Put the pastry on a 28 x 38cm (11 x 15in) baking sheet, and roll lightly with a rolling pin to smooth down the pastry. Score lightly around the edge, to create a 3cm (1¼ in) border.

2 Put the apple slices on top of the pastry, within the border. Turn the edge of the pastry halfway over, so that it reaches the edge of the apples, then press down and use your fingers to crimp the edge. Dust heavily with icing sugar.

3 Bake in the oven for 20–25 minutes until the pastry is cooked and the sugar has caramelised. Serve warm, dusted with more icing sugar.

Serves 8	EASY		NUTRITIONAL INFORMATION	
	Preparation Time 10 minutes	Cooking Time 20-25 minutes	Per Serving 221 calories, 12g fat (of which 0g saturates), 29g carbohydrate, 0.4g salt	Vegetarian

125g (4oz) short-grain pudding rice

1.1 litres (2 pints) full-fat milk

4 tbsp golden caster sugar

grated zest of 1 small orange

2 tsp vanilla extract

whole nutmeg to grate

Rice Pudding

1 Preheat the oven to 180°C (160°C fan oven) mark 4. Lightly butter a 900ml (1½ pint) ovenproof dish. Add the pudding rice, milk, sugar, orange zest and vanilla extract, and stir everything together. Grate a little nutmeg all over the top of the mixture.

2 Bake the pudding in the oven for 1½ hours or until the top is golden brown, then serve.

Serves	EASY		NUTRITIONAL INFORMATION	
6	**Preparation Time** 5 minutes	**Cooking Time** 1½ hours	**Per Serving** 235 calories, 7g fat (of which 5g saturates), 35g carbohydrate, 0.2g salt	Vegetarian Gluten free

Baked Apples

125g (4oz) hazelnuts
125g (4oz) sultanas
2 tbsp brandy
6 large Bramley apples, cored
4 tbsp soft brown sugar
100ml (3½ fl oz) apple juice
thick cream to serve

1 Preheat the oven to 190°C (170°C fan oven) mark 5. Spread the hazelnuts over a baking sheet and toast under a hot grill until golden brown, turning them frequently. Put the hazelnuts in a clean teatowel and rub off the skins, then chop the nuts. Put to one side.

2 Soak the sultanas in the brandy and set aside for 10 minutes. Using a small sharp knife, score around the middle of the apples to stop them from bursting, then stuff each apple with equal amounts of brandy-soaked sultanas. Put the apples in a roasting tin, and sprinkle with the brown sugar and apple juice. Bake in the oven for 15–20 minutes until soft.

3 Serve the apples with the toasted hazelnuts and a dollop of cream.

EASY		NUTRITIONAL INFORMATION		Serves
Preparation Time 5 minutes, plus 10 minutes soaking	**Cooking Time** 15–20 minutes	**Per Serving** 280 calories, 13g fat (of which 1g saturates), 36g carbohydrate, 0g salt	Vegetarian Gluten free • Dairy free	**6**

Bread and Butter Pudding

400g (14oz) panettone, cut into 1cm (½ in) slices,
then diagonally in half again to make triangles

4 medium eggs

450ml (¾ pint) milk

3 tbsp golden icing sugar

1 Preheat the oven to 180°C (160°C fan oven) mark 4. Arrange the slices of panettone in four 300ml (½ pint) gratin dishes or one 1.1 litre (2 pint) dish.

2 Beat the eggs, milk and 2 tbsp of the sugar in a bowl, and pour over the panettone. Soak for 10 minutes.

3 Put the puddings or pudding in the oven, and bake for 30–40 minutes. Dust with the remaining icing sugar to serve.

Serves 4	EASY		NUTRITIONAL INFORMATION	
	Preparation Time 10 minutes, plus 10 minutes soaking	**Cooking Time** 30–40 minutes	**Per Serving** 450 calories, 13g fat (of which 5g saturates), 70g carbohydrate, 1.1g salt	Vegetarian

Glossary

Al dente Italian term commonly used to describe foods, especially pasta and vegetables, which are cooked until tender but still firm to the bite.

Baking blind Pre-baking a pastry case before filling. The pastry case is lined with greaseproof paper and weighted down with dried beans or ceramic baking beans.

Baste To spoon the juices and melted fat over meat, poultry, game or vegetables during roasting to keep them moist. The term is also used to describe spooning a marinade over food.

Beat To incorporate air into an ingredient or mixture by agitating it vigorously with a spoon, fork, whisk or electric mixer. The technique is also used to soften ingredients.

Bind To mix beaten egg or other liquid into a dry mixture to hold it together.

Blanch To immerse food briefly in fast-boiling water to loosen skins, such as peaches or tomatoes, or to remove bitterness, or to destroy enzymes and preserve the colour, flavour and texture of vegetables (especially prior to freezing).

Bouquet garni Small bunch of herbs – usually a mixture of parsley stems, thyme and a bay leaf – tied in muslin and used to flavour stocks, soups and stews.

Braise To cook meat, poultry, game or vegetables slowly in a small amount of liquid in a pan or casserole with a tight-fitting lid. The food is usually first browned in oil or fat.

Caramelise To heat sugar or sugar syrup slowly until it is brown in colour; ie forms a caramel.

Chill To cool food in the fridge.

Compote Fresh or dried fruit stewed in sugar syrup. Served hot or cold.

Coulis A smooth fruit or vegetable purée, thinned if necessary to a pouring consistency.

Cream To beat together fat and sugar until the mixture is pale and fluffy, and resembles whipped cream in texture and colour. The method is used in cakes and puddings which contain a high proportion of fat and require the incorporation of a lot of air.

Croûtons Small pieces of fried or toasted bread, served with soups and salads.

Crudités Raw vegetables, usually cut into slices or sticks, typically served with a dipping sauce.

Curdle To cause sauces or creamed mixtures to separate, usually by overheating or over-beating.

Cure To preserve fish, meat or poultry by smoking, drying or salting.

Deglaze To heat stock, wine or other liquid with the cooking juices left in the pan after roasting or sautéeing, scraping and stirring vigorously to dissolve the sediment on the bottom of the pan.

Dice To cut food into small cubes.

Dredge To sprinkle food generously with flour, sugar, icing sugar etc.

Dust To sprinkle lightly with flour, cornflour, icing sugar etc.

Escalope Thin slice of meat, such as pork, veal or turkey, from the top of the leg, usually pan-fried.

Fillet Term used to describe boned breasts of birds, boned sides of fish, and the undercut of a loin of beef, lamb, pork or veal.

Flake To separate food, such as cooked fish, into natural pieces.

Folding in Method of combining a whisked or creamed mixture with other ingredients by cutting and folding so that it retains its lightness. A large metal spoon or plastic-bladed spatula is used.

Fry To cook food in hot fat or oil. There are various methods: shallow-frying in a little fat in a shallow pan; deep-frying where the food is totally immersed in oil; dry-frying in which fatty foods are cooked in a non-stick pan without extra fat; see also Stir-frying.

Garnish A decoration, usually edible, such as parsley or lemon, which is used to enhance the appearance of a savoury dish.

Gluten A protein constituent of grains, such as wheat and rye, which develops when the flour is mixed with water to give the dough elasticity.

Griddle A flat, heavy, metal plate used on the hob for cooking scones or for searing savoury ingredients.

Gut To clean out the entrails from fish.

Hull To remove the stalk and calyx from soft fruits, such as strawberries.

Infuse To immerse flavourings, such as aromatic vegetables, herbs, spices and vanilla, in a liquid to impart flavour. Usually the infused liquid is brought to the boil, then left to stand for a while.

Julienne Fine 'matchstick' strips of vegetables or citrus zest, sometimes used as a garnish.

Macerate To soften and flavour raw or dried foods by soaking in a liquid, eg soaking fruit in alcohol.

Marinate To soak raw meat, poultry or game – usually in a mixture of oil, wine, vinegar and flavourings – to soften and impart flavour. The mixture, which is known as a marinade, may also be used to baste the food during cooking.

Medallion Small round piece of meat, usually beef or veal.

Mince To cut food into very fine pieces, using a mincer, food processor or knife.

Parboil To boil a vegetable or other food for part of its cooking time before finishing it by another method.

Pare To finely peel the skin or zest from vegetables or fruit.

Poach To cook food gently in liquid at simmering point; the surface should be just trembling.

Pot-roast To cook meat in a covered pan with some fat and a little liquid.

Purée To pound, sieve or liquidise vegetables, fish or fruit to a smooth pulp. Purées often form the basis for soups and sauces.

Reduce To fast-boil stock or other liquid in an uncovered pan to evaporate water and concentrate the flavour.

Refresh To cool hot vegetables very quickly by plunging into ice-cold water or holding under cold running water in order to stop the cooking process and preserve the colour.

Roast To cook food by dry heat in the oven.

Roux A mixture of equal quantities of butter (or other fat) and flour cooked together to form the basis of many sauces.

Rubbing in Method of incorporating fat into flour by rubbing between the fingertips, used when a short texture is required. Used for pastry, cakes, scones and biscuits.

Salsa Piquant sauce made from chopped fresh vegetables and sometimes fruit.

Sauté To cook food in a small quantity of fat over a high heat, shaking the pan constantly – usually in a sauté pan (a frying pan with straight sides and a wide base).

Scald To pour boiling water over food to clean it, or loosen skin, eg tomatoes. Also used to describe heating milk to just below boiling point.

Score To cut parallel lines in the surface of food, such as fish (or the fat layer on meat), to improve its appearance or help it cook more quickly.

Sear To brown meat quickly in a little hot fat before grilling or roasting.

Seasoned flour Flour mixed with a little salt and pepper, used for dusting meat, fish etc., before frying.

Shred To grate cheese or slice vegetables into very fine pieces or strips.

Sieve To press food through a perforated sieve to obtain a smooth texture.

Sift To shake dry ingredients through a sieve to remove lumps.

Simmer To keep a liquid just below boiling point.

Skim To remove froth, scum or fat from the surface of stock, gravy, stews, jam etc. Use either a skimmer, a spoon or kitchen paper.

Steam To cook food in steam, usually in a steamer over rapidly boiling water.

Steep To immerse food in warm or cold liquid to soften it, and sometimes to draw out strong flavours.

Stew To cook food, such as tougher cuts of meat, in flavoured liquid which is kept at simmering point.

Stir-fry To cook small, even-sized pieces of food rapidly in a little fat, tossing constantly over a high heat.

Sweat To cook chopped or sliced vegetables in a little fat without liquid in a covered pan over a low heat to soften.

Tepid The term used to describe temperature of approximately blood heat, ie 37°C (98.7°F).

Vanilla sugar Sugar in which a vanilla pod has been stored to impart its flavour.

Whipping (whisking) Beating air rapidly into a mixture either with a manual or electric whisk. Whipping usually refers to cream.

Zest The thin, coloured outer layer of citrus fruit, which can be removed in fine strips with a zester.

Index